The Just Shall Live By Faith

The Just Shall Live By Faith

An Expanded Outline Commentary
on the Book of Romans

DAVID PAUL McDOWELL

Foreword by Nicholas Perrin

WIPF & STOCK · Eugene, Oregon

THE JUST SHALL LIVE BY FAITH
An Expanded Outline Commentary on the Book of Romans

Wipf & Stock
An Imprint of Wipf and Stock Publishers
199 W. 8th Ave., Suite 3
Eugene, OR 97401

www.wipfandstock.com

PAPERBACK ISBN: 978-1-7252-5269-1
HARDCOVER ISBN: 978-1-7252-5270-7
EBOOK ISBN: 978-1-7252-5271-4

Manufactured in the U.S.A.   02/13/20

Contents

Foreword

FREDERICK L. GODET, ONE of the leading New Testament scholars of the nineteenth century, once called Romans "the cathedral of the Christian faith." He was right of course. From the moment you walk through the vast door of Paul's prologue in chapter 1, to the moment you cross the transept of Romans 12:1, until you walk out the back door of Paul's closing benediction (Rom 16:25–27); it *is* a cathedral from start to finish. I have to imagine that when Godet penned this thought, his mind's eye was recalling the cathedral of his own hometown, the *Collegiale* of Neuchâtel, a looming medieval edifice graced with interior beauty and external spires reaching to the sky. As it is with the *Collegiale*, so it is with our epistle: Romans' compelling logic and delicate beauty astonish us, even as it directs our hearts heavenward in worship. Like a cathedral, Romans is a world unto itself, reflecting upon a new reality wrought by God through Jesus Christ.

Having visited more than a few cathedrals over the years, I have often found these enduring architectural wonders to be daunting—even overwhelming. You walk in and almost instantly grasp its vastness, beauty, and antiquity. But as you move up and down the aisles, you do so with either increasing briskness or increasing slowness. On the one hand, if you find yourself picking up the pace of your tour, it's probably because you realize that you don't have the capacity to grasp all of that the art and architecture was intended to mean, and as a result you begin to lose the thread in one big blur. On the other hand, you might be one of those visitors who slows down after a short while. You slow down perhaps for the same reason: there's just too much to take in and there's nothing to do except to take a load off your feet and think about where to eat lunch.

Paul's epistle can have the same effect on many of its readers. You've heard all the hype about Romans; you've read the great "blurbs" from major thinkers like Augustine, Luther, and Calvin; but you're not sure you're seeing what they're seeing. More exactly, you're not sure you're seeing what you think you're *supposed* to be seeing. You start out reading or even teaching through Romans and then, before you know it, you find yourself moving more and more quickly (or get more and more bogged down in the details) because you're not sure what to do with all that information.

As a tourist (not just at cathedrals but also other places), I've noticed that the thing that sets good tour guides apart from "just okay" tour guides is their ability to keep the main thing the main thing. Sure, the local Swiss experts could probably tell you all kinds of fascinating if not random factoids about the *Collegiale*, and those things may be interesting for a few of the more eager sightseers. But for the rest of us, we don't want the comprehensive architectural tour: we want a concise explanation that also has wings.

Likewise, for *most* of us reading Romans, we do not necessarily need an expert who can tell us every nuance of every Greek word. Nor do we need a set of bullet points handed to us like abstracted bullet points. Instead, we want a tour guide to walk us down the most important aisles, show us the most important sculpture pieces, give us the "flow" of the room—all the while keeping it conversational, real and lively. Accessibility without oversimplification is hard to come by in the vast world of commentaries.

So, if you are asking, "Do we really need another commentary on Romans?" For my money, the answer is "Yes." In fact, we need a commentary just like this one, for all the reasons I've touched upon. In fact, if Romans is really as important as the Reformers and countless theologians have been telling us for centuries, then it will always require a slow but steady influx of fresh-eyed tour guides who understand the *pastoral needs* of today's church as well as the text. I would submit that this commentary is just such a commentary.

Sometimes when I visit a medieval European cathedral, I marvel at the contrast between the extraordinary, and sometimes centuries-long efforts that went into constructing the edifice and the relatively slight interest in those same buildings today. Now I don't know what attendance at the *Collegiale* was like in the thirteenth century, but I would wager that its current attendance pales in comparison with its earliest beginnings. One asks, "What happened? What went wrong?" Though I would not presume to answer this question with full confidence, I do have at least one personal theory: that somehow or other the church failed to faithfully interpret, expound, and translate the precious truths of Romans. And because the church somewhere along the line failed to so, the gospel of God ceased to be relevant. To put this differently, the reason why so many cathedrals today seem more like museums than houses of worship is not because the church lacked the Scriptures, but because the church neglected to re-proclaim the gospel afresh in its own time.

It is impossible to re-proclaim the gospel without first rediscovering it. And it is impossible to rediscover it without sage guides walking us 'round the cathedral. But again: it's not just information that we're after but how it's presented. The modern church's fervent hope and prayer is that today's mostly empty cathedral will be tomorrow's hotbeds of gospel proclamation. And if that aspiration is fulfilled, I am certain that we will have to credit, in part, commentaries like this one. To quote Godet one more time (along with our author below): "The probability is that every great revival in the church will be connected as effect and cause with a deeper understanding of this book."

Once commentators have done their part in faithfully exegeting and applying the text, it remains for readers to pick up and read. Of course Romans wasn't written simply to be read, but to be believed and then to be proclaimed. Whether the reader of the present volume fancies himself or herself as merely a reader, or perhaps a believer, or perhaps again a proclaimer, there's something for everyone in these pages. At the same time, we must keep in mind that when Paul wrote this epistle over two thousand years ago, he wrote it with a vision that his literary cathedral might lay the basis for the church at Rome. The reason we need to read and reread Romans again and again in our own day is because the charter document for the church at Rome has for all intents and purposes proven to be the foundational text of the universal church.

Gentle reader, as you go forward with this commentary, I invite you to read carefully and thoughtfully. Why? Because how one responds to this "cathedral of the Christian faith" in one's own life and understanding will have direct impact on the on-going construction of the cathedral that will last forever.

NICHOLAS PERRIN
President, Trinity International University

Introduction

WHY ANOTHER COMMENTARY ON Romans? Very simple: I wanted to write one. I taught a course on Romans for sixteen years at the Berkshire Institute for Christian Studies in Lenox, Massachusetts. I never tired of teaching its compelling message (although some of my students might have tired of my teaching). There is a reality about this book that makes it contemporaneous with any age. There is also a certain pathos, a depth and height of experience that makes it the *Les Misérables* of biblical literature. Seldom is the degradation of the human condition revealed in such startling detail—like ripping a tuxedo off a corpse. And rarely is one confronted by the sheer brilliance of God's grace available to all who believe in Jesus Christ, regardless of racial affinity or moral poverty. The experiential impact on the lives of so many throughout history is sufficient reason to immerse oneself in the study of this book. Here are just a few examples of this impact (some of the following material is found in John Stott's commentary on Romans:[1]

AUGUSTINE

Under great conviction of sin, he sat weeping in the garden of a friend, unable to make a break with his old life of sexual addiction. He heard a child singing "Tolle, Lege! Tolle, Lege!" ("Take up and read"). Taking the scroll of the Scriptures, he read Romans 13:13–14. He said, "No further would I read

---

1. Stott, *Romans*, 20–24.

nor had any need; instantly, at the end of this sentence, a clear light flooded my heart and all the darkness of doubt vanished away."[2]

MARTIN LUTHER

Commenting on Romans 1:16–17; "At last, by the mercy of God, meditating day and night, I gave heed to the context of the words, namely, 'In it the righteousness of God is revealed, as it is written, He who through faith is righteous shall live.' There I began to understand that the righteousness of God is that by which the righteous lives by a gift of God, namely by faith. And this is the meaning: the righteousness of God is revealed by the gospel, namely, the passive righteousness with which a merciful God justifies us by faith . . . Here I felt that I was altogether born again and had entered paradise itself through open gates."[3]

JOHN WESLEY

On May 24, 1738, John Wesley was at a meeting where a person was reading the preface to Luther's commentary on Romans. "I felt my heart strangely warmed. I felt I did trust in Christ, Christ alone, for my salvation; an assurance was given me that He had taken my sins away, even mine; and saved me from the law of sin and death."[4] Wesley's life launched the Evangelical revival of the eighteenth century in England.

DUMITRU CORNILESCU

While studying at the Orthodox Seminary in Bucharest, he was translating the Bible into modern Romanian and came to Romans. He saw that God in Christ had done everything necessary for our salvation. "I took this forgiveness for myself; I accepted Christ as my living Savior."[5] His translation was finished in 1921; he was exiled by the Orthodox Patriarch in 1923 and died some years later in Switzerland.

---

2. Augustine, *Conf.* 8.29.
3. Luther, "Preface to Latin Writings," 337.
4. Wesley, *Journal*, 103.
5. Stott, *Romans*, 22.

FREDERICK L. GODET

"The probability is that every great revival in the church will be connected as effect and cause with a deeper understanding of this book."[6]

JOHN CALVIN

"When anyone gains a knowledge of this Epistle, he has an entrance opened to him to all the most hidden treasures of Scripture."[7]

F. F. BRUCE

"Time and again in the course of Christian history it [Romans] has liberated the minds of men, brought them back to an understanding of the essential Gospel of Christ, and started spiritual revolutions."[8]

JOHN STOTT

"Paul's letter to the Romans . . . remains a timeless manifesto . . . of freedom through Jesus Christ. It is the fullest, plainest and grandest statement of the gospel in the New Testament. Its message is not that man was born free . . . but rather that human beings are born in sin and slavery and that Jesus Christ came to set us free."[9]

There is another reason for this commentary. We live in an era of history that has been designated as post-modern, the era following modernity—a period from 1789 to 1989, from the Enlightenment to the fall of Communism. Within this post-modern era there are great numbers of people who have become the soulless legacy of the scientific and technological displacement of religion. Such hollow men and women have experienced the terrible ennui of human autonomy as a consequence of "letting God go" and they are left to decide what is right and wrong not by reason but by how they feel. I believe they long for hope, something authentic, and

---

6. Godet, *Commentary on Romans*, 12.
7. Calvin, *Commentaries on Acts, Romans*, xxiv.
8. Bruce, "Epistle to the Romans," 160.
9. Stott, *Romans*, 19.

something greater than themselves that will put the pieces of their broken world together, bringing healing and order. Though they may not know it, they have a deep longing for a relationship with the God of grace who has revealed himself in Jesus Christ.

The book of Romans magnifies the beauty of God's initiating love for those at enmity with him. The book also addresses the reason for the alienation and aloneness of the postmodern existential predicament; it espouses the value of community; it helps distinguish genuine Christianity from a tradition-encrusted version; and it offers certainty and solidity in the face of an amorphous and wispy spirituality.

It is my hope that this commentary will be greatly used by churches and serious students of the Bible. This commentary was not written for the classroom, but from a pastoral perspective to be used in small group study. This is the reason why it is laid out in outline form instead of chapters with questions at the end of each major section; for the purpose of individual response and group interaction.

May God richly bless the efforts of your journey through Romans as he has all those pilgrims who have gone before you.

DAVID MCDOWELL
West Chicago

PART ONE

Chapters 1–11

I

Paul Greets the Church at Rome (1:1–15)

IN VERSES 1–7, PAUL gives an opening salutation that is longer than in any other of his epistles. John Murray suggests that it is because Rome was the only church that he did not found or had not visited.[1] Ernst Kasemann also suggests that since he was unknown to this Roman congregation, Paul had to officially introduce himself.[2] Paul begins with a characteristic Hellenistic opening which consisted of identifying the person who wrote the letter as well as to whom the letter was written, followed by a greeting.

> Paul, a bondservant of Jesus Christ, called to be an apostle, separated to the gospel of God, which He promised before through His prophets in the Holy Scriptures, concerning His Son Jesus Christ our Lord, who was born of the seed of David according to the flesh, and declared to be the Son of God with power according to the Spirit of holiness, by the resurrection from the dead. Through Him we have received grace and apostleship for obedience to the faith among all nations for His name, among whom you also are the called of Jesus Christ; to all who are in Rome, beloved of God, called to be saints: Grace to you and peace from God our Father and the Lord Jesus Christ. (vv. 1–7)

1. Murray, *Epistle to the Romans*, 1.
2. Kasemann, *Commentary on Romans*, 3.

In this paragraph (which is one very long sentence in the Greek New Testament) Paul characterizes himself as a slave (*doulos*) of Christ. Schreiner suggests that this term is rooted in the Old Testament concept of the *'ebed yhwh* (the servant of the Lord), and that Paul saw himself as continuing the work of Moses, Joshua, David, and the other prophets.[3] If this is his meaning, then Paul acknowledges his apostolic authority as a derived authority having a continuity with the work of God in the Old Covenant. Far from flaunting this authority, Paul endeavored to fulfill his lofty calling and divine commission to preach to the gentiles as a humble servant of Jesus Christ, chosen and saved by the grace of God.

Unfolded in his introduction are the important themes that we will see Paul develop in the rest of the book: "the gospel that is of God," that focuses on the Son, that is designed to bring all nations to the obedience of faith and is never seen by Paul as contradictory to the Old Testament; "the obedience of faith" (*eis hypakoen pisteos*), which implies that faith in Christ is not a libertinism but that which brings real transformation in those who believe; "the grace of God," which provides a Savior and initiates the free offer of the gospel to sinful, alienated humanity deserving judgment; and "peace with God," which characterizes the status of the one who is justified by grace through faith.

The centerpiece of Paul's gospel is Jesus Christ, whose praises are sung in verses three and four in hymn-like fashion, which might have been an early confessional formula. Since Paul is introducing himself to Christians in Rome, he wants to underscore his basic doctrinal agreement with those he desires to visit (and perhaps convince to be a part of his proposed missionary venture to Spain). He begins his confessional about Jesus by displaying his own Jewish roots. He presents the Davidic descent of Christ, which was an essential qualification of the Messiah according to Jewish understanding. Thus according to his human nature, Jesus was the "Son of David." Some early commentators see here an implication of the preexistence of the Son.

> As he is truly God, so is he truly man. For he would not be truly man if he were not of flesh and soul. Otherwise he would be incomplete. For though he was the Son of God in eternity, he was not known by the creation until, when God wanted him to be revealed for the salvation of mankind, he made him visible and corporal, because God wanted him to be known through his power to

---

3. Schreiner, *Romans*, 32.

cleanse humans from their sins by overcoming death in the flesh. Therefore he was made the seed of David.[4]

The earthly lineage of Christ does not exhaust his identity. He was also "declared to be the Son of God with power according to the Spirit of holiness, by the resurrection from the dead." In spite of his apparent ordinariness according to human nature, Christ's resurrection brought "an investiture with power"[5] that demonstrated his true glory. Jesus was always the Son of God but was not declared to be the Son of God with power until his resurrection. This is underscored more vividly in the NIV, which preserves the word order of the Greek text and places "Jesus Christ our Lord" at the very end of verse four so that it reads "and who through the Spirit of holiness was declared with power to be the Son of God by his resurrection from the dead: Jesus Christ our Lord."

This power, which manifested Christ as our Savior and our God, is none other than the Spirit of holiness or the Holy Spirit. For it is by the power of the Holy Spirit that the believer is enabled to live a holy life. Paul makes this connection in Romans 8:8–11 and most poignantly in Ephesians 1:19–20, where Paul prays that the church would be enlightened to know that the very same Spirit who raised Christ from the dead is at work in them.

> Paul is affirming . . . that the One who has always been God's Son but was brought by His human birth into a relationship with David as far as His human nature is concerned, was appointed the glorious Son-of-God-in-power from the time of His resurrection—a fact which is attested by the present sanctifying work of the Holy Spirit in believers.[6]

Kasemann calls verses 1–7 a prescript and verses 8–15 a proem (preliminary comment). Schreiner divides the introduction into the Salutation (vv. 1–7) and the Thanksgiving (vv. 8–15). Call it what you will, Paul moves from the doctrinal to an expression of thanksgiving and prayer for the Roman Christians, as well as revealing his hopes for a coming visit.

> First, I thank my God through Jesus Christ for you all, that your faith is spoken of throughout the whole world. For God is my

---

4. See Bray, *Ancient Christian Commentary*, 7 for a quote from Ambrosiaster's *Commentary on the Epistle to the Romans*.

5. Hendriksen, *Romans*, 32

6. Cranfield, *Romans*, 7.

witness, whom I serve with my spirit in the gospel of His Son, that without ceasing I make mention of you always in my prayers, making request if, by some means, now at last I may find a way in the will of God to come to you. For I long to see you, that I might impart to you some spiritual gift, so that you may be established—that is, that I may be encouraged together with you by the mutual faith of both you and me. Now I do not want you to be unaware, brethren, that I often planned to come to you (but was hindered till now), that I might have some fruit among you also, just as among other Gentiles. I am a debtor both to Greeks and to barbarians, both to wise and unwise. So, as much as is in me, I am ready to preach the gospel to you who are in Rome also. (vv. 8–15)

This is not merely polite rhetoric. Paul believed the church at Rome to have a genuine faith even though he was not the one who led them to it. Paul may have had some issues but he was never territorial when it came to the gospel. "What then? Only that in every way, whether in pretense or in truth, Christ is preached; and in this I rejoice, yes, and will rejoice" (Phil 1:18). He was grateful that God had extended the gospel to Rome most likely through the pilgrims from Rome who had been in Jerusalem and had heard Peter's sermon at Pentecost (Acts 2:10). As the apostle to the gentiles, he had a passion to see Christ proclaimed to the unreached places of the earth. Paul even believed that these Christians would be an encouragement to him, which demonstrates that a good minister of the gospel must be willing to receive as well as to give. In verse 9, *gar* (for) is a link between his thanksgiving and prayer, and Paul's desire to visit the Romans. All of these are expressions of his apostolic function.[7]

Many commentators have weighed in on Paul's motive for wanting to visit Rome. Suffice it to say that the church at Rome was the only church in the gentile world that did not have an apostolic foundation. I do not think that Paul was jealous of this fact, yet because he was called to the gentiles and was "a debtor both to Greeks and to the barbarians," he indicates in verses 11–12 that there were reasons for his desire to visit. First, he wanted *to impart some spiritual gift* to the Romans so that they might be established or strengthened in their faith. (When I first wrote this, my wife was in Turkey using *her* spiritual gift in order to encourage and strengthen a woman from our church who was serving in that part of the world.) Second, Paul wanted "to preach the gospel to you who are in Rome also." He wanted to exercise his apostolic function of preaching the gospel, which

7. Schreiner, *Romans*, 49.

does not merely mean the initial work of bringing folks to Christ but also of encouraging them and strengthening them in the faith. Could it be that the preaching of the gospel designed to encourage and strengthen is the content of this very letter of Romans?

> The Roman Christians needed to understand the Pauline Gospel, which proclaims the unity of Jews and Gentiles in Christ. By grasping this union . . . the Roman community would dissolve the divisions plaguing them. Paul hopes that by imparting his understanding of the gospel to them they will be strengthened for the cause of the gospel and support him in his mission to Spain. The spiritual gift must be understood then as the apostolic gift. As the Apostle to the Gentiles, Paul desires the Romans to comprehend his gospel to the Gentiles and to be strengthened by it.[8]

There is a third reason for Paul's visit, which is revealed much later in the letter (15:24). He had reached a significant point in his ministry where he was looking for new frontiers in which to do his missionary work, so he had a vision to go to Spain. Paul's philosophy of missions was not to bring everyone to a knowledge of the gospel as much as it was to bring the knowledge of the gospel everywhere. In other words, he brought the gospel to an area and he left it up to others to spread that gospel around in that area while he went somewhere else. He planned on visiting Rome after he presented a money offering which he collected from the gentile churches in Asia Minor for the struggling mother church of Jerusalem. He hoped that the Romans would support him in his new missionary venture. (Good background material on how all these plans transpired can be found in Acts 21:17—28:30.) By God's grace, Paul went to Rome but he would never reach Spain.

---

8. Fee, *God's Empowering Presence*, 487–88.

II

Paul's Theme: Equal Acceptance by God For Jew and Gentile through Justification by Faith (1:16–17)

Review

WE BELIEVE THAT THE apostle Paul was the author of this letter, written near the end of his third missionary journey from Corinth, most likely 56 to 59 AD. It was written to the church at Rome, which he had never visited but wanted to prepare for his coming in the near future on his way to a new missionary venture to Spain. Some scholars, like T. W. Manson, believe that Paul's letter to the Romans may have originally ended with chapter fifteen, to which he attached chapter sixteen and sent the whole letter to the church at Ephesus.[1]

Preview

Paul was writing to a church composed of Jews and gentiles. He had received information that there were problems, divisions, misunderstandings

---

1. Donfried, *Romans Debate*, 13.

of the gospel and a real confusion as to how each cultural group fit into the covenant of grace. Originally, the church at Rome was predominately Jewish, perhaps founded by European Jews who had heard the gospel preached in their own language at Pentecost (Acts 2:10). However, many Jews were expelled from Rome around 49 AD by Emperor Claudius and therefore the church became predominately gentile.

This Jew/gentile issue is incredibly important to the understanding of Romans because it creates the fabric into which Paul weaves his two major themes:

1. The justification of the guilty sinner by grace through faith in Christ alone. This is the great leveling device between Jew and gentile, for both are equally guilty before God and both are equally saved by faith in Christ, apart from culture and religion. (It is important to reiterate that Paul's understanding of justification, though individual in its application, also has social and ecclesiological relevance for the unity of Jew and gentile in one church through the preaching of one gospel.)

2. The redefinition of the people of God not based upon physical lineage or ethnic origin, but simply through faith in Christ. Thus Jew and gentile are equal as one people before God because of Christ, yet without discounting the ancient promises to Israel.

Let's look at this first major theme of Romans, found in 1:16–17.

> For I am not ashamed of the gospel, for it is the power of God for salvation to everyone who believes, to the Jew first and also to the Greek. For in it the righteousness of God is revealed from faith to faith, as it is written, "The righteous shall live by faith." (ESV)

Why did Paul begin so negatively? Perhaps it is because there is a "sober recognition of the fact the gospel is something of which . . . Christians will be constantly tempted to be ashamed."[2] Rome was the center of human wisdom and power, and when confronted with the gospel, human instinct would consider such teaching as foolish and weak in comparison. There is also a sense in which the very nature of the gospel is not replete with the trappings of wealth, power, and wisdom; that one needs to lay aside dependence on all those things which service our ambitions and to humble oneself before God. Paul, however, was not ashamed of the gospel and saw through the charade of what the world valued. "For the message of the cross

2. Cranfield, *Romans*, 17.

is foolishness to those who are perishing, but to us who are being saved it is the power of God" (1 Cor 1:18).

Martin Luther was very clear on this:

> We therefore come to the following conclusion: he who believes in the gospel must become weak and foolish before men, so that he may be strong and wise in the power and wisdom of God, as it is written in I Corinthians 1:17, 25. When you therefore observe that the power of God can be readily rejected, let this be a sign of the power of the flesh and the world. This is why all power, wisdom, and righteousness are hidden and buried and not apparent, in accordance with the image and likeness of Christ, who emptied himself in order to hide completely his power, wisdom, and goodness, disclosing only his weakness, foolishness, and harsh suffering. In a similar way, one who is powerful, wise, and at ease must have these goods as if he did not have them. That is why the life of the princes of this world and of the lawyers is a most dangerous one, because they must maintain themselves by power and knowledge. . . . For it is difficult to despise and hide from one's own esteem what everyone regards highly.[3]

The reason why Paul is not ashamed of the gospel is because he considers it the power of God, *dunamis theou*. There are three major Greek words for power: *kratos*—power to rule, dominion (e.g. technocrat, democrat); *exousia*—authority, right (John 1:12); *dunamis*—explosive strength (dynamite). It is this last word for power that Paul chose to use here. In the face of the power of Greek learning and intelligence, the gospel is the explosive power that confounds and makes foolish the wisdom of the world. In the face of the crushing power of the Roman military machine to conquer and destroy, the gospel is the explosive power that raises men from the dead and changes the human heart.

Human wisdom and power may get a person far along in this "dog-eat-dog" world of ours, but they cannot solve the deeper issues of one's human existence. No amount of learning can change a heart of hatred and prejudice into a heart of love. No amount of power (physical, material, political) can bring contentment or satisfaction. They leave us hungry for the real thing.

Thus, Paul is not ashamed of the gospel for it is the power of God that saves people, changes people, and restores the *imageo dei,* which has been defaced by human sin. Paul's understanding of salvation is based upon the Hebrew *shalom:* a condition or state of healthiness of soul and spirit in

3. Luther *Commentary on Epistle to the Romans,* 17.

relationship to God. Salvation is not a "one-shot deal" that comes through a decision in the past. Rather, salvation is a present-tense relationship with God that decisively separates us from our past, creates for us a new present, and gives us a future hope. This power to change us, to be radically different than in the past, is available to anyone who believes in Jesus Christ. This is the great equalizing phrase and central motif: "to everyone who believes, first for the Jew and then for the Gentile." Historically, the gospel came originally to the Jews and then through the Jews the gospel came to those who are gentiles, without disenfranchising the Jews. This gospel has universal applicability because it is to be received through simple faith.

What, then, is this powerful gospel about which Paul wrote? Verse 17: "For in the gospel, a righteousness from God is revealed" (NIV). Most people think that righteousness is the moral quality of being perfect or holy, something we generate and hope that God accepts. Martin Luther had such an understanding at first. He saw the righteousness of God as God's perfect standard by which he judged all imperfection. Such an understanding drove him farther from God because of his awareness that God was absolutely perfect and he was a sinner. However, Paul spoke not of a righteousness of human achievement but one of God's gracious initiative whereby he puts the sinner *in the right* and clears the guilty of all condemnation simply by his grace. Robert Haldane writes,

> God has provided . . . a righteousness—the complete fulfillment of the law in all its threatenings and all its precepts—by which, being placed on our account though faith, (we are) acquitted from guilt, freed from condemnation, and entitled to the reward of eternal life.[4]

A Jew might have interpreted all this as a call to covenant faithfulness. "Being in the right" might mean obeying the law and carrying out covenant commitments. However, the next phrase tells us how this right-standing with God is achieved; "a righteousness that is by faith from first to last, just as it is written, 'The righteous shall live by faith'" (NIV). Paul quotes from Habakkuk 2:4 and takes significant freedom to interpret the connection between faith and righteousness. In other words, right-standing with God comes not through our efforts to be righteous, but through God's gracious initiative to give us righteousness through faith in Christ. Martin Luther, in his 1515 *Commentary on Romans*, described the impact of this verse,

4. Haldane, *Romans*, 48–49.

"Night and day I pondered it . . . until I grasped the truth that the righteousness of God is that righteousness whereby, through sheer grace and mercy, He justifies us by faith."[5] This was a radical departure from the Roman Catholic understanding of justification as sanctification—an infusion of righteousness. However, Luther's study of the term revealed a *declarative* and *forensic* definition. Justification by faith is defined, therefore, as "the legal act of God by which He declares the sinner righteous on the basis of the perfect righteousness of Jesus Christ."[6]

> Luther saw in this the very essence of Christian Theology. God reached down not halfway to meet us in our vileness but all the way down, to the foul dregs of our broken humanity. And this holy and loving God dared to touch our lifeless and rotting essence and in doing so underscored that this is the truth about us. In fact, we are not sick in need of healing. We are dead in need of resurrecting. We are not dusty and in need of a good dusting; we are fatally befouled with death and fatally toxic filth and require total redemption. If we do not recognize that we need eternal life from the hand of God, we remain in our sins and eternally dead.[7]

There was a powerful scene in the 1953 classic film "Martin Luther," directed by Irving Pichel and starring Niall MacGinnis. (The movie was nominated for two Oscars.) Luther was a priest and a professor in the Roman Catholic Church. He had been studying the book of Romans and was becoming convinced that one's acceptance by God was not based upon the merit of good works, but upon Christ's completed work on the cross. This was not accepted Roman Catholic theology. In this particular scene, Luther was standing behind a man who was the head of the Augustinian order and who had just returned with a large quantity of relics. Relics were the remains of some saint or martyr, which when venerated produced an indulgence—the forgiveness in part of the guilt of one's sin and shortening of one's purgatorial punishment. As his superior was displaying the relics to the adoring crowd, Luther walked out in frustration. His superior later found him in his study. They debated the place of relics and Luther showed him what he had been studying in Romans 1:17. At one point, his superior said that if one took away relics and other holy things, which he claimed

5. Luther, *Romans*, 25.
6. Berkhof, *Systematic Theology*, 517.
7. Metaxis, *Martin Luther*, 97.

were aids to faith, what would one have left? Luther answered, "Christ; man only needs Jesus Christ!"

Our only hope is that we are in the right with God. Such hope comes not on the basis of our efforts, but on the basis of faith alone, by grace alone, in Christ alone.

III

Universal Guilt of Humanity (1:18—3:20)

A. THE GUILT OF THE GENTILE (PAGAN) WORLD (1:18-32)

Review

AFTER A BASIC INTRODUCTION and an announcement of a proposed visit to Rome on his way to Spain, the apostle Paul declared the theological essence of his great Epistle to the Romans: that in the gospel, "the righteousness of God has been revealed from faith to faith." In other words, "being in the right" with God has been provided for anyone who believes the gospel, the good news of Jesus' death and resurrection, regardless of one's ethnic origin or religious affiliation. "As it is written, the just shall live by faith." Thus we conclude that a person is rescued from spiritual death and eternal alienation from God not by the best efforts of the human soul but by grace alone, through faith alone, in Christ alone.

Preview

Instead of proceeding with a greater explanation of justification by faith (he picks up this theme later in 3:21), Paul has some necessary groundwork to lay by setting forth the *need* of God's gracious initiative in salvation. He has to tell us the bad news before we can grasp how good the good news is. In 1:18—3:20, Paul solemnly declares the reality of a world guilty as sin before God and therefore under his wrath. This section plays itself out like a huge courtroom scene, where God is the judge and Paul the prosecuting attorney. Paul calls up before the bar of God's justice three categories of humanity and proves each to be guilty: the gentile (pagan) world, the moral world, and the religious world. In the section before us, we will look at the first category: the pagan world under the wrath of God (1:18–32).

What is the wrath of God? 1:18: *'Apokaluptetai gar orge theou ap' oupanou.* "For the wrath of God is revealed from heaven." The wrath of God is an essential concept in the book of Romans. The wrath of God is heaven's response to human sin.[1] It is the steady, determined disposition of the Creator toward the rebellion of his creatures. It is *not* vengeful or resentful (or else the word *thumos* would have been used), but it is the settled condition of judgment and estrangement that results from sinful humanity crashing into the perfect nature of a holy God. Paul says, "the wrath of God is revealed" (*apokaluptetai*), which is the same root word as "Revelation," the last book of the New Testament. So the wrath of God has something to do with the final judgment brought into the present—"the wrath of God is revealed."

Why is the wrath of God being revealed? 1:18b–19: "against all ungodliness [*asebeian*] and unrighteousness [*adikian*] of men who suppress [*katexonton*] the truth in unrighteousness, because what may be known of God is manifest in them, for God has shown it to them." How? See 1:20–21a: "For since the creation of the world His invisible attributes are clearly seen, being understood by the things that are made, even His eternal power and Godhead, so that they are without excuse, because, although they knew God they did not glorify Him as God, nor were they thankful."

The charge by Paul, the prosecuting attorney, is threefold: *ungodliness* (attitudes and actions hostile to God); *unrighteousness* (wicked attitudes and actions that are hostile to humanity); and *suppression of the truth*, the truth of God's existence, thereby failing to glorify and honor him. Paul is using a

---

1. Dunn, *Romans*, 54.

15

typical Jewish apologetic here when he claims that the sin of paganism does not lie in a lack of knowledge but in the breaking of the first commandment.[2]

"Objection, your Honor," the defense might respond. "How could my clients be guilty of suppressing the truth about God when they did not know anything about God in the first place? After all, they are the heathen world; they never had a Bible in their language, never had a church in their culture, and never heard the gospel of Jesus Christ. How can they be accused of willfully suppressing the truth? Why, even the famous philosopher Bertrand Russell, when asked what he would say to God in order to justify his atheism, said, 'I will tell him he did not give me enough evidence.'[3] We plead ignorance!"

Paul, the prosecuting attorney, responds: "Your Honor, it is true that they did not have the special revelation of Scripture and the gospel, but they did have a kind of revelation in the form of their own conscience and in the evidence of Creation" (Ps 19:1–6). If they had looked within themselves, they would have recognized the natural capacity to believe in a higher power that exists in all humanity; and if they had looked around, they would have seen the fingerprints of God all over his Creation. "God has stitched into the fabric of the human mind his existence and power, so that they are instinctively recognized when one views the created world."[4]

"Your Honor, they may not have had enough evidence to give them the knowledge of salvation, but God has woven enough evidence into them and around them to render them accountable for not honoring or gratefully serving their Creator." The issue is they don't *want* God to exist, so they can live as they please. They are without excuse. According to Paul, rebellion is the "signature of human reality" apart from Christ.[5]

A modern example of this rebellious refusal comes from Thomas Nagel, professor of Philosophy at New York University: "I want atheism to be true and am made uneasy by the fact that some of the most intelligent and well-informed people I know are religious believers. It isn't just that I don't believe in God and naturally hope there is no God! I don't want there to be a God; I don't want the universe to be like that."[6]

---

2. Kasemann, *Commentary on Romans*, 42.

3. Zacharias, *Jesus among Other Gods*, 47.

4. Schreiner, *Romans*, 86.

5. Kasemann, *Commentary on Romans*, 42.

6. Zacharias, *Jesus among Other Gods*, 50.

The central point of this passage is that the root sin of humanity, against which the wrath of God has been revealed, is the failure to glorify God and to give him thanks. The righteousness of God is rooted in a desire to honor and glorify his Name. Those who are justified by faith, who have the righteousness of God applied to them, are those who live to glorify the Name of God. True worship is the enactment of the First Commandment: "I am the Lord your God. . . . You shall have no other gods before Me" (Exod 20:3). Our response is to acknowledge God as the Ultimate One, who is worthy of our praise, adoration, and gratitude, for it is from him that all blessings flow. Worship is also an acknowledgment that while there are other truths and concerns in life, none take precedence over him who is the Truth. Those who do not acknowledge God in such a way are under the wrath of God, not merely for being sinners, but for failing to render due honor and glory to their Creator. As we will see, all sin flows from the fountain of this sin.

How is God's wrath revealed?

1. Verse 21: Failure to glorify God leads to human reasoning becoming corrupt. "Although they knew God, they did not glorify Him as God, nor were thankful, but became futile in their thoughts, and their foolish hearts were darkened." Paul changes the verbs from active to passive in order to begin this section on the consequences of this rebellion: futility (*mataioo*, without result or success) in one's imagination (*dialogismos*, self-deliberation), and foolishness (*asunetos*, without understanding) in one's heart (*kardia*, the seat of feeling, intelligence, and moral choice). Someone has said that moral choices are no longer made based on reason, but based upon feelings. This is an apt description of how humanity thinks apart from God.

Sir Isaac Newton had worked for days on his scientific inquiries into the nature of the universe. He worked in a small room by candlelight and by him sat his faithful dog. Newton left the room for just a moment and the dog jumped up to follow him, and in the process knocked over the candle onto his notes, setting them ablaze and rendering them a pile of ashes. When Newton returned and saw what had happened, his heart was broken and he wept. The dog came over and put his head on his master's lap. Newton stroked the dog's head and gently said, "You will never, never know what you have done."[7]

---

7. Zacharias, *Jesus among Other Gods*, 36.

Man apart from God is clueless to the real significance of life and the consequences of his actions. The one who breaks free of God becomes a slave of futility. "He becomes incapable of discriminating perception, loses any grasp of reality, and falls victim to illusion."[8] I think that this is an apt description of some of our modern entertainment, especially the proliferation of reality TV. Such programming not only illustrates the boredom of our culture, but also vividly portrays the hunger for vicarious life experiences which have little to do with reality and that flows from a futile mind and a foolish heart. Truly, when we fail to glorify God our minds and emotions are affected.

2. Verses 22–23: Failure to glorify God and having a debased mind leads to the creation of an alternative spirituality (idolatry). "Professing to be wise, they became fools, and changed the glory of the incorruptible God into an image made like corruptible man, and birds and four-footed animals and creeping things." Thus, breaking the second commandment follows transgressing the first: "You shall not make for yourself a carved image" (Exod 20:4). We might not relate to Paul's description of idolatry in the ancient world but we can understand the principle that "man is incurably religious" and he must worship something. When we exchange the truth about God for a lie, we do not become atheists, we become the creators of our own religion or brand of spirituality complete with relics to worship and venerate: career, money, sex, food, drugs, children, health, TV, and pornography.

Robert Jewett has written a very interesting work on tolerance in a pluralistic culture. His premise is that tolerance requires that the tension between the first two commandments be preserved: tolerance without faith violates the Second Commandment, giving rise to relativism and nihilism; faith without tolerance violates the First Commandment, producing a zealous fanaticism.

> In a sense, the First Commandment is the chief guardian of genuine humanity, a hedge against persons becoming arrogant enough to think they are gods, which, if the Garden of Eden story is to be taken to its full theological depth, is the perennial story of the fall of the human race. The constant danger of tolerance without faith is that it falls into such relativistic malaise, encouraging the raising of personal preference to the point of ultimate concern. When this

8. Kasemann, *Romans*, 44.

happens, the social fabric rips, and no limits are left. Social chaos is the long-term result, and tolerance itself is an inevitable casualty.[9]

3. Verses 24–25: Failure to glorify God leading to idolatry also results in the dishonoring of our bodies. "Therefore God also gave them up to uncleanness, in the lusts of their heart, to dishonor their bodies among themselves, who exchanged the truth of God for a lie, and worshiped and served the creature rather than the Creator, who is blessed forever. Amen." Paul uses the phrase "gave them over" (*paradidomi*, to give over into one's power or use), which he repeats in verses 26 and 28. God's wrath has already broken out, however, he has not consigned sinners to hell but to their own sin.[10] When a culture (or a person) lets God go, God lets them go. What a terrible judgment. To be left alone to the consequences of my own choices while I continue to cave in upon myself! Paul affirms the Jewish polemic that false worship led to moral depravity by stating the close connection between idolatry and sexual sin. We can see this throughout the Old Testament as well as in the paganism of the first century. Idolatry was often sexualized so that the act of intercourse became a part of the ritual of worship of a deity.

But there is a greater principle here: we become like the object of our worship. "The man who worships beasts is not devoured by them, but becomes like them."[11] If we create a god out of our own imagination, then the standard for right and wrong will come from the same place. If we trash the truth about the Creator God, then we will trash the parameters that he has set up for proper sexual conduct. We will laugh at the beauty of virginity; ridicule the commitment to chastity; stigmatize marital faithfulness as an impossible ethic; normalize divorce and minimize its effects upon children. We will also be a culture that, in the name of freedom, dishonors and abuses our bodies and the fruit of our bodies—our children.

4. Verses 26–27: Failure to glorify God also leads to dishonorable passions. "For this reason God gave them over to vile passions. For even their women (*thelus*) exchanged (*metallasso*) the natural use (*chresis*) for what is against nature (*phusis*). Likewise also the men (*arsen*), leaving the natural use of the woman, burned in lust for one another, men with men committing what is shameful, and receiving in themselves the penalty of their error which was due." Just as idolatry is unnatural in view of the true God, so the

9. Jewett, *Christian Tolerance*, 78–79.
10. Barrett, *Epistle to the Romans*, 38.
11. Barrett, *Epistle to the Romans*, 38.

practice of homosexuality is unnatural in view of the true God's created order (*phusis*, the laws and order of nature).

More liberal commentators have reinterpreted Paul at this point. They believe that Paul's use of *natural* and *unnatural* has to do with whether those who engage in homosexual activity are heterosexual by "nature" or homosexual by "nature." In other words, they say that Paul was speaking against the conduct of heterosexuals engaged in homosexual activity (man-boy sex and ritual prostitution). For these, such activity was against their natures as heterosexuals. Surely, they would say, Paul had nothing to say against those who are "born" homosexual and are involved in committed loving homosexual relationships. They argue that Paul was a product of his age and wasn't aware of this phenomenon.

On the contrary, the issue is not whether Paul was culturally naïve about sexual orientation. From his perspective, the sinner was never separated from his sin, and there is no indication that Paul considered homosexuality a greater manifestation of sinful nature than he did adultery, slander, gossip, and greed (1:29–30). The real issue here is to understand what Paul meant when he used the words *natural* and *unnatural*. The context refers to God as Creator and the evidence of his existence by the created order. Therefore, nature or natural refers to that which God originally intended for sexual union—one man, one woman, for one lifetime. Anything that deviates from this plan is against nature, or *unnatural*. This also goes for heterosexual and other sexual activity outside the parameters of God's original design for marriage.

There was not a feature of pagan society that filled the Jew of Paul's day with such loathing as the toleration of homosexual practice. However, to Paul such activity was dishonorable because it was "that perversion of the created order which may be expected when men put the creation in place of the Creator. That idolatry has such consequences is to Paul a plain mark of God's wrath."[12] Paul is talking about homosexual behavior, not same sex-attraction. There are Christians who are *same-sex attracted*, but who have not identified as gay/lesbian nor have chosen to act upon that attraction. Rather, their journey of discipleship traverses the pathway of celibacy and their desire for intimacy motivates them to seek deep friendships within the body of Christ and a more robust theology of singleness.

5. Verses 28–32: Failure to glorify God also leads to a debased mind where everything becomes possible. "And even as they did not retain God

12. Barrett, *Epistle to the Romans*, 39.

in their knowledge, God gave them over to a debased mind, to do the things which are not fitting." Paul goes on to describe these inappropriate behaviors as five vices ("filled with all . . . unrighteousness, sexual immorality, wickedness, covetousness, maliciousness"); five more vices ("full of . . . envy, murder, strife, deceit, evil-mindedness"); eight kinds of inappropriate people ("whisperers, backbiters, haters of God, violent, proud, boasters, inventors of evil things, disobedient to parents"); and five virtues, all of the Greek words beginning with a prefix meaning "no," indicating what these idolaters lack ("no discernment, no trustworthiness, no love, no forgiveness, and no mercy"). In addition, Paul maintains his original charge that these people have suppressed the truth in that they knew God's laws and yet continued to do wrong and encourage others to do the same.

Karl Barth summarizes the downward progression of evil in this section by noting that a damaged eye may lead to blindness and defective knowledge can become ignorance of God.

> [These people] "become no longer capable of serious awe and amazement. They become unable to reckon with anything except feelings and experiences and events. . . . Here is the final vacuity and disintegration. Chaos has found itself, and anything may happen. The atoms swirl, the struggle for existence rages. Even reason becomes irrational. . . . The world is full of personal caprice and social unrighteousness—this is not a picture merely of Rome under the Caesars! The true nature of our unbroken existence is here unrolled before us. Our ungodliness and unrighteousness stand under the wrath of God. His judgment now becomes judgment and nothing more; and we experience the impossibility of men as the real and final impossibility of God."[13]

What is the result? "The end of our wandering in the night is death."[14] We are deserving of death (Rom 1:32)! We are under the wrath of God (Rom 1:18)! Paul spares no one who is outside Jesus Christ. However, neither will Paul spare the good news, that God in his mercy has provided a way of escaping his own wrath. God is "not willing that any should perish but that all should come to repentance" (2 Pet 3:9).

13. Barth, *Epistle to the Romans*, 54–55.
14. Barth, *Epistle to the Romans*, 55.

B. THE GUILT OF THE MORAL WORLD (2:1–16)

Review

The apostle Paul functions as the prosecuting attorney in the trial of the century. He tries to prove that the whole world is guilty before God and deserving of the wrath of God. All of this "bad news" or "negative talk" forms the background to the really positive "good news" of God's grace, which Paul introduces in 1:16–17 and will reintroduce in 3:21. The first segment of sinful humanity that Paul brings before the bar of God's justice, is the gentile world (1:18–32), which has suppressed the truth of God's existence and failed to give God the honor and glory that is his due as Creator. God's wrath is displayed against this segment of humanity by letting them go (1:24, 26, 28) to do whatever their evil hearts desire. This has produced a downward cultural spiral manifested by the futility of thinking, the creation of alternative systems of spirituality, sexual baseness, and a whole list of inappropriate actions that flow from a debased mind.

Preview

Paul now turns his sights to the prosecution of a second segment of humanity known as the moral world. Such moral people, whether from Jewish or gentile backgrounds, would certainly have agreed with Paul's assessment of paganism. However, Paul quickly accuses them of the same sins for which they have so vehemently judged the pagan world. Once again, the theme is the judgment of God.

God's Judgment Is Universal (2:1–4)

> Therefore you are inexcusable, O man, whoever you are who judge, for in whatever you judge another you condemn yourself; for you who judge practice the same things. But we know that the judgment of God is according to truth against those who practice such things. And do you think this, O man, you who judge those practicing such things, and doing the same, that you will escape the judgment of God? Or do you despise the riches of His goodness, forbearance and longsuffering, not knowing that the goodness of God leads you to repentance?

It is interesting to note that Paul switches from the third-person plural in chapter 1 to the second-person singular in this passage. He addresses an imaginary individual whom he calls "O man," or in some translations "Sir." Paul isn't just talking to himself, although some commentators believe that he was speaking against a kind of strict Jewish morality, which he had experienced in his pre-Christian days. Paul is using an ancient polemical style that interacted with an imaginary person known as an *interlocutor*. Socrates used such a device in most of his diatribes. Paul's interlocutor represents the moral Jew or gentile who would naturally distance himself from the vices of the pagan world and would say "Amen" to everything Paul said in the previous passage.

F. F. Bruce uses an example of the Stoic philosopher Seneca, the tutor of the Emperor Nero and a contemporary of Paul. "Seneca might have listened to Paul's indictment (of the Pagan World) and said, 'Yes, that is perfectly true of the great masses of mankind, and I concur in the judgment which you pass on them—but there are others, of course, like myself, who deplore these tendencies as much as I do.'"[15]

Bruce goes on to show how Seneca espoused the great moral virtues of the ancient world and even preached against idolatry. Yet, in contrast to all he proclaimed, he was a coconspirator with Nero in the murder of the emperor's mother Agrippina. Here is an example of a "moral" gentile, who proclaimed judgment upon the immoral world and yet committed immoral actions himself. One could think of an example from the Jewish world as well: Herod the Great (a half-Jew), who built the grand temple in Jerusalem and was a very capable ruler, yet killed his own wife, drowned his brother-in-law (the high priest), and strangled three of his own sons out of jealousy. The emperor Augustus Caesar reportedly used a play-on-words and said, "I'd rather be Herod's pig [Gr. *hus*] than his son [Gr. *huios*]."[16] As Herod lay dying, he ordered that all Jewish leaders be brought to his sports arena (the Hippodrome) and kept there until he died. At the news of his death, the archers were to execute these leaders so that all Judea would mourn his death. Thankfully, the archers never carried out the order. This was the same Herod who also ordered the slaughter of babies in Bethlehem around the time of Christ's birth and it was carried out. Here was a "moral" Jew who ruled well, cared for the poor, relieved his people of heavy taxation

15. Bruce, *Letter of Paul to the Romans*, 86
16. Macrobius, *Saturnalia* 2:4, 11.

in a time of famine, yet was filled with jealously and rage to the extent of murdering his own family and killing innocent children.

There is another example with which we may more easily identify. Remember when you were younger and your brother annoyed you and harassed you until you couldn't take it anymore, so you smacked him? Whom did your parents punish? You, because they saw you hit him. "It's not fair," you screamed. "Tough," they said. "Go to your room." So you endured the punishment, feeling angry, hurt, and what else? Self-righteous! In your desire for justice to be heaped upon your sibling, you completely overlooked your own sin. This is the hypocrisy of the double standard that is often expressed by having a high standard for others and then lowering the bar for ourselves.[17]

We might point our fingers at the sexual predators in our culture and wish they would be locked away or strung up so that they would no longer take advantage of our young. However, what of the hatred and bitterness that we display in our vitriolic criticism of these individuals? Should we think that the judgment of God would fall on them for their sexual sins and not upon us for the murderous hatred in our hearts? We may criticize those who are homosexual and stand for gay marriage, but what of the secret heterosexual sins that lurk in our own hearts, making us adulterers or pornographers in the sight of God? Do we think that God has a certain standard of judgment for other people and another standard for us? "All of us have sinned; we have all fallen short of God's glory" (Rom 3:23). Let us not suppose that our good fortunes in life—our cars, money, homes, good health, or popularity are signs of God's approval. They may indeed indicate God's patience, not his blessing, in giving us time to repent.

God's Judgment Is Perfectly Just (2:5–11)

> But in accordance with your hardness and your impenitent heart you are treasuring up for yourself wrath in the day of wrath and revelation of the righteous judgment of God, who will render to each one according to his deeds: eternal life to those who by patient continuance in doing good seek for glory, honor, and immortality; but to those who are self-seeking and do not obey the truth, but obey unrighteousness—indignation and wrath, tribulation and anguish, on every soul of man who does evil, of the Jew

17. Stott, *Romans*, 82.

first and also of the Greek; but glory, honor, and peace to everyone who works what is good, to the Jew first and also to the Greek. For there is no partiality with God.

Paul makes some profound accusations of his interlocutor, Mr. Moralist. Instead of repentance characterizing his life, the moralist is desensitized to his sin; he just doesn't see it. His condition is one of hardness, stubbornness of heart (*sklerotes*), and impenitence (*ametanoetos*). The moralist's sin has desensitized him from feeling the need of repentance, while at the same time making him more judgmental of others for the same sin. Here is a word picture: a man with huge calluses on his hand is leaning on a hot stove yelling at his child to stop playing with matches. He is sensitive to his child playing with fire but does not even know that his own hand is burning. Paul warns the moralist that he is in dreadful danger—far more than the burning of his hand. He is treasuring up (*thesaurizeis*) for himself the wrath of God and not his blessing.

There are three things to note about the judgment of God in 2:5–6:

1. It is a righteous judgment that will be revealed. The decision of judgment will not be made at the end of human history, as one would await the decision of a jury. Rather, the process of God's judgment is taking place right now and will be fully revealed in the day of judgment. (See Romans 1:18, John 3:36, 1 Corinthians 1:18 for evidence that unbelievers are already under the wrath of God.)

2. It is a righteous judgment of God that is based upon a standard with which every moral person would agree. It is a standard found in Psalm 62:12: You render to a man according to his work (ESV).[18] It may sound like Paul is contradicting what he said about justification by faith (1:16–17), but in the context, a judgment according to our deeds is exactly what he means. God is going to demonstrate why a portion of humanity will be given eternal life and another portion will be given death. He will do this by showing that we have either lived for the glory of God and his honor or we have lived for ourselves (self-seeking ambition) and have not obeyed the truth.

3. It is a righteous judgment of God that is applied equally to all; to the Jew first and also to the gentile. No doubt Paul's Jewish audience would have been astounded, and not a little annoyed, that Paul placed them

18. Also see these passages: Matt 16:27; 25:31–36; 2 Cor 5:10; Gal 6:5; Eph 6:8; Col 3:24; Rev 2:23; 20:12.

on the same level of judgment with gentiles. And the moral gentiles would have been offended that they were placed on the same level of judgment as the immoral gentiles. God is not a judge who can be manipulated into showing favoritism to people according to ethnic origin. He cannot be bribed or bought by our vain attempts at morality or religion.

God's Righteous Judgment Is Based on a Fair Standard (2:12–16)

> For as many as have sinned without the law will also perish without the law, and as many as have sinned in the law will be judged by the law (for not the hearers of the law are just in the sight of God, but the doers of the law will be justified; for when Gentiles, who do not have the law, by nature do the things in the law, these, although not having the law, are a law to themselves, who show the work of the law written in their hearts, their conscience also bearing witness, and between themselves their thoughts accusing them or else excusing them) in the day when God will judge the secrets of men by Jesus Christ, according to my gospel.

The best way to unpack this passage is to notice that verses 13–16a are parenthetical. Go back now and read the three verses outside the parentheses, verses 12 and 16. Can you express Paul's thought in your own words? God will judge everyone according to the law (standard of behavior) under which they have lived. It doesn't say that those innocent people who have never heard about the Bible or the gospel will be saved. This passage has to do with judgment, not salvation. It does say that everyone's sin will be revealed by the very standard by which they have chosen to live.

What about the meaning of Paul's statement inside the parentheses? Everyone has some knowledge of God's law written upon the heart, no matter how darkened or marred because of sin. And our conscience bears witness to the validity of this law, either approving or condemning certain behavior.[19] It is the work of this conscience that will find its fulfillment in the final judgment of God. In other words, God's judgment will not tell you anything that you don't already know about yourself. It will only reveal that which you have kept secret.

19. Schreiner, *Romans*, 123.

Let me conclude by means of an illustration adapted from Francis Schaeffer in in his book *The Church at the End of the Twentieth Century*.[20] Let us suppose that every baby born into this world received a small digital recorder that he wore around his neck throughout his entire life. This recorder only recorded one thing: any moral statement made about someone else. For those brought up in a Judeo-Christian-Islamic culture, these moral judgments would be based upon the law of God found in a holy book. For those brought up in another culture—religious or tribal—their judgments would be made based upon what they or their culture felt to be right and wrong. So this person goes through his entire life recording his own moral statements about others and finally dies. He stands before God as his judge and God reaches down and pushes the play button on his recorder. What the person hears is his own voice judging others by the standards most familiar to him. Then God simply asks, "Have you lived up to the standards of your own moral judgments?" Every one of us will be condemned, not by God, but by the words of our own mouths. Paul says in Romans 3:19 that "every mouth will be stopped, and the whole world may be held accountable to God!" (ESV).

We need a savior! "For God did not send His Son into the world to condemn the world, but that the world through Him might be saved" (John 3:17). At the end of human history, Jesus will be the judge. During these days of grace, he has come to save.

> What will you do with Jesus? Neutral you cannot be.
>
> For one day you will be asking, "what will He do with me?"

C. THE GUILT OF THE JEWISH WORLD AND THE REDEFINITION OF A TRUE JEW (2:17—3:8)

Review

The apostle Paul, functioning as the prosecuting attorney in the trial of the century, strives to prove that the whole world is guilty before God and deserving of the wrath of God. Paul has so far turned his sights to the prosecution of the pagan world and to a second segment of humanity known as the moral world.

20. Schaeffer, *Church*, 49.

Preview

Paul now turns his attention to the guilt of the religious world. These are the people who proudly base their certainty of God's favor upon their nationality and meticulous observance of their code of conduct. However, Paul will contend that their observance of the law (moral and ceremonial) is an outward observance and that the ethnic advantage of being a Jew is nullified by their spiritual transgression of the law.

> Indeed you are called a Jew, and rest on the law, and make your boast in God, and know His will, and approve the things that are excellent, being instructed out of the law, and are confident that you yourself are a guide to the blind, a light to those who are in darkness, an instructor of the foolish, a teacher of babes, having the form of knowledge and truth in the law. (vv. 17–20)

Here Paul for the first time addresses the ethnic Jew directly who would certainly see himself in contrast to those whom Paul mentioned in verses 14–16. He lists the great privilege they have in being Jews: they are proud of their very name, they rest or rely upon the law given by God, they boast about their covenantal relationship with God, they know God's will (because they have God's word), they approve the things that are excellent (able to discern the best and most significant things), and are qualified to be the instructors of others who lack such discernment (like the gentiles). What a privileged position!

However, Paul puts forth the accusation:

> You, therefore, who teach another, do you not teach yourself? You who preach that a man should not steal, do you steal? You who say, "Do not commit adultery," do you commit adultery? You who abhor idols, do you rob temples? You who make your boast in the law, do you dishonor God through breaking the law? For "the name of God is blasphemed among the Gentiles because of you," as it is written. (vv. 21–24)

It is almost as if Paul sets them up and then pulls the rug out from under them. By means of several rhetorical questions he basically tells them that they have failed to live up to the very advantage they have as Jews— they are hypocrites! They have set up a system of externalized righteousness, which has served as a cover for their underlying theft, adultery, and sacrilege. Paul's words echo those of Jesus in the Sermon on the Mount, but especially Matthew 23, even down to the expressions *blind guides* and *blind fools.* Perhaps this is why the Pharisees were called "the smooth ones" by the Qumran community.

The most powerful accusation is the one that Paul takes from God's word, most likely from Isaiah 52:5 in the Septuagint; "God's Name is blasphemed among the Gentiles because of you." Some have seen Ezekiel 36:20 as forming a part of Paul's thought here, but I agree with Schreiner[21] that the Isaiah passage is more consistent with Paul's argument, which he continues:

> For circumcision is indeed profitable if you keep the law; but if you are a breaker of the law, your circumcision has become uncircumcision. Therefore, if an uncircumcised man keeps the righteous requirements of the law, will not his uncircumcision be counted as circumcision? And will not the physically uncircumcised, if he fulfills the law, judge you who, even with your written code and circumcision, are a transgressor of the law? For he is not a Jew who is one outwardly, nor is circumcision that which is outward in the flesh; but he is a Jew who is one inwardly; and circumcision is that of the heart, in the Spirit, not in the letter; whose praise is not from men but from God. (vv. 25–29)

Paul rehearses the obvious: physical circumcision was central to the very nature of being a Jew. It was a God-given sign which sealed his covenant and which distinguished the Jew from the nations. It was also a requirement if one was to convert to Judaism. However, Paul upends the obvious and argues that circumcision only has value if one is a law-keeper, not a law-breaker. "But it was not a magical ceremony or charm. It did not provide them with permanent insurance over against the wrath of God."[22]

Paul is not saying anything revolutionary. The Old Testament contained such an indictment (Deut 10:16; 30:6; Jer 4:4) and proclaimed the need to circumcise the heart and not merely carry out the requirements of the law as an external rite. "For he is not a Jew who is one outwardly" (*en to phanero*, "in the open"). What is shocking is the way Paul applies the spiritual principle of circumcision by saying that those who keep the law's commands and yet are physically uncircumcised (gentiles) will be regarded as if they were the people of God. "But he is a Jew who is one inwardly [*en to krypto*, "in secret"]; and circumcision is that of the heart, in the Spirit, not in the letter." Not only will these gentiles be regarded as God's people, but they will judge those who are law-breaking Jews.

21. Schreiner, *Romans,* 134.
22. Stott, *Romans,* 92.

I do not believe that Paul is advocating that anyone can be saved by keeping the law. He will make that very clear in the rest of his letter. However, I agree with Schreiner that Paul is speaking here of the Christian Jew or gentile whose obedience to the law is not salvific, but flows out of his faith in Jesus Christ.[23] Such a situation is made possible because of the promise of a new heart that God will give his people in the New Covenant (Ezek 44:9; Jer 9:25; Ezek 36:26).

In summation, Paul serves up a crushing blow to spiritually bankrupt Judaism. He actually redefines who is a Jew and at the same time makes a play on the word "Jew," which means "praise." The Jew boasted of his birth and trusted in the external rites, expecting the "praise" of men (Matt 6:5; John 5:44). However, what is necessary is the circumcision of the heart, which entails an inward work of the Spirit and earns "praise" from God. In addition, Paul says that being an ethnic Jew complete with circumcision is not only *not* necessary to belonging to the people of God, but could cause greater condemnation for not keeping what they know to be the law's requirements. Once again this should not be seen as revolutionary, but as the fulfillment of Old Testament prophecy stating what God would do in the last days when he would pour out his Spirit upon all flesh.

Barrett[24] suggests at this point that Paul imagines himself face to face with a Jewish "heckler" who argues with the accusations Paul has made. However, Stott believes that "Paul the Pharisee and Paul the Christian are in debate with each other, as in Philippians 3."[25] Thus the one objects by asking four questions and the other answers each objection. To help clarify this, I have italicized the objections and the answers are in normal print with quotation marks:

What advantage, then, is there in being a Jew, or what value is there in circumcision? "Much in every way! First of all, the Jews have been entrusted with the very words of God." *What if some were unfaithful? Will their unfaithfulness nullify God's faithfulness?* "Not at all! Let God be true, and every human being a liar. As it is written: 'So that you may be proved right when you speak and prevail when you judge.'" *But if our unrighteousness brings out God's righteousness more clearly, what shall we say? That God is unjust in bringing his wrath on us? (I am using a human argument.)* "Certainly not! If that were so, how could God judge the world?" *Someone*

23. Schreiner, *Romans*, 139–40.
24. Barrett, *Epistle to the Romans*, 43.
25. Stott, *Romans*, 95.

might argue, "If my falsehood enhances God's truthfulness and so increases his glory, why am I still condemned as a sinner?" Why not say—as some slanderously claim that we say—"Let us do evil that good may result"? "Their condemnation is just!" (3:1–8, NIV)

We could list these objections and answers in this way:

Objection 1: If outward circumcision is not as important as "circumcision" of the heart, is there any advantage to being an ethnic Jew?

Answer 1:   Yes! You have been made the very custodians of the word of God! What a great honor!

Objection 2: However, what if Israel has proven unfaithful to that trust? Does that nullify God's promises to Israel?

Answer 2:   No! Israel's unfaithfulness does not frustrate God's purposes. In fact, our unfaithfulness hallmarks God's truth. (A more complete answer to this question is articulated at length in chapters 9–11.)

Objection 3: Well, if my unfaithfulness brings out God's faithfulness more clearly and my sin establishes his righteousness, then why should I be punished? I'm actually helping God out.

Answer 3:   That is foolish! How can God be the moral ruler of the universe if he did not punish sin? Whenever God judges sin he is justified in doing so (Ps 51:4).

Objection 4: This is an extension of objection 3. C. H. Hodge describes this argument: "the worse we are, the better; for the more wicked we are, the more conspicuous will be the mercy of God in our pardon."[26] (Another version of this argument is repeated in chapter 6, verse 1.)

Answer 4:   It is unclear whether Paul refers to the argument or the people who make this argument; either way, he strongly condemns it (or them).

Thus the object of this entire section is complete. Paul has effectively argued that Jews are sinners and lawbreakers, as are the gentiles (pagan and moral), and cannot be justified before God by their ethnicity or by their works. They may have had a superior advantage in being guardians of God's word, but they have proven unfaithful to that very word even though God remained

26. Hodge, *Commentary on Romans*, 75.

faithful to them. However, because God is righteous, he will not countenance any justification for human sin. He must justly condemn all flesh.

D. UNIVERSAL GUILT BEFORE GOD IN THAT NO ONE WILL BE DECLARED RIGHTEOUS BY KEEPING THE LAW (3:9–20)

Review

Paul has systematically accused the entire human race as guilty before God and deserving of his wrath. He has brought forth evidence to back up his accusations against the pagan world complete with its idolatry and perversion, the moral world complete with its empty moralism, and the religious world with its hypocrisy and ethnic chauvinism.

Preview

Here we have the closing arguments of Paul, the prosecuting attorney, who literally diagrams the depravity, the pervasiveness, and the universality of the guilt of the human race; so that "every mouth may be silenced and the whole world held accountable to God" (3:19). As he speaks our heads droop lower and lower until we see the strawberry jam on our shirts and know that we have been exposed and there is nothing we can say or do. Let us look at verses 9–20 (NIV):

> What shall we conclude then? Do we have any advantage? Not at all! For we have already made the charge that Jews and Gentiles alike are all under the power of sin. As it is written:
>
> "There is no one righteous, not even one; [Eccl 7:20]
> there is no one who understands;
> there is no one who seeks God." [Ps 14:2]
> "All have turned away, they have together become worthless;
> there is no one who does good, [Ps 14:1–3]
> not even one." [Ps 53:1–3]
> "Their throats are open graves;
> their tongues practice deceit." [Ps 5:9]
> "The poison of vipers is on their lips." [Ps 140:3]

"Their mouths are full of cursing and bitterness." [Ps 10:7, 15–17]
"Their feet are swift to shed blood;
ruin and misery mark their ways,
and the way of peace they do not know." [Isa 59:7; Prov 1:16]
"There is no fear of God before their eyes." [Ps 36:1]

The word "sin" is a theological term and not just a moral one. It is, first and foremost, a reference to our relationship with God and that is why when a public official breaks the law, we bring him or her before an ethics committee and not a sin committee. From a faith perspective, sin is always against God. David confessed his sin of adultery by saying, "Against You alone have I sinned and done this evil in Your sight" (Ps 51:4). Paul uses the word forty-nine times in the book of Romans and it is found for the first time here in verse 9. There are several Greek words which define a variety of expressions for man's sinful response to God:

- Overstepping a boundary: *parabaino*—to transgress or go beyond a boundary; we have crossed the line and deviated from the right pathway into territory where we do not belong.

- Breaking the law: *paranomia*—lawlessness, sometimes translated iniquity.

- Crooked or bent: *skolios*—morally crooked or perverse; we live in a bent and crooked world; some of us may look straighter when compared to other bent sticks, but when compared to the perfectly straight edge of the law, we are all very bent indeed.

- Defiance: *anomia*—disregard for God's laws.

- Ungodly: *asebeia*—disregard for God's Person, impious.

However, the word used here in verse 9 is *harmartia*; it means missing the mark. God has placed a target before us, a standard of righteousness and holiness that one must meet in order to be in a right relationship with him; no one has been able to reach it: "for all have sinned and fallen short of the glory of God" (Rom 3:23). Paul mentions that religious people like the Jews may have some advantage—you might be baptized, catechized, immunized, and pasteurized, but these cannot deal with your sin or shield you from God's wrath. Religious people, just like the rest of humanity, have not only fallen short of the glory of God reflected in the law, but have fallen under the rule and enslavement of sin as a governing principle. "Paul thought that sin had wrapped its tentacles so tightly around human beings that they could not keep the law."[27]

Thus Paul launches into a biblical catena to illustrate his point. It is almost like an x-ray of the human condition. I know I'm mixing metaphors jumping from a law court to a medical model, but look at the figure below.

X-RAY OF THE HUMAN CONDITION UNDERS SIN

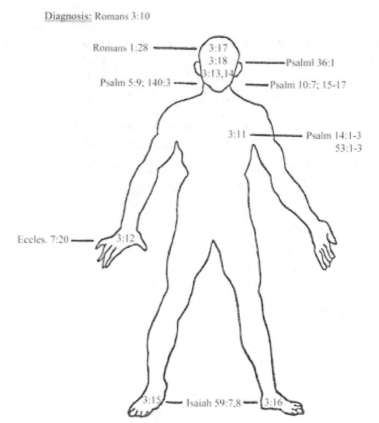

Diagnosis: Romans 3:10

Romans 1:28 ——— 3:17
3:18 ——— Psalm 36:1
3:13,14

Psalm 5:9; 140:3 ——— Psalm 10:7; 15-17

3:11 ——— Psalm 14:1-3
53:1-3

Eccles. 7:20 ——— 3:12

3:15 — Isaiah 59:7,8 — 3:16

Prognosis: Romans 3:19-20

27. Schreiner, *Romans*, 164.

You will see that most of the verses from Romans 3 are placed inside the figure and the citations from the Old Testament Septuagint on the outside of the figure. Taken together they depict the pervasiveness, the barbarity, and the power of sin. Our condition is so grave that it affects our minds, eyes, throats, tongues, mouths, lips, hearts, feet, hands, lifestyles, and relationships.

Now, in response to this, one might say, "Pastor, wait a minute. Most of us here cannot relate to the vicious and revolting symptoms of sin in this figure. We are cultivated people with consciences who don't do things like this. Many of us were brought up in religious or highly moral families and while we're not perfect (who is?), we're not that sick."

What about verse 11? "No one seeks God" (taken from Psalm 14:1–3), which means we do not make God's glory our chief concern. See also Psalm 10:4, which says that "in all our thoughts there is no room for God," or that we have not done what Jesus said was the very essence of the law—we do not love him at all times "with our heart, soul, mind, and strength, and our neighbor as ourselves."

"Pastor, be realistic; I've got to live my life in this world with all of its stresses and distractions. You don't really expect me to think of God all the time. Do you?"

No, I don't, and that is exactly why I am also guilty before God. This is the very crux of our sickness—the very root of sin; a self-centered existence where the whole world shrinks to the size of our puny lives; where therapy is more important than theology, happiness more important than righteousness, and feelings more important than truth;[28] where even our best thoughts of God are few and far between, and our most overwhelming experiences of his glory in worship are swallowed up by lunch or the opening kickoff. And everything we do flows out of this self-enclosed vacuum that once had been filled by God. We are now shadows of what we were created to be. We are not only fallen but we are broken. We who were created with such vast capacities for imaging God have become the carriers of corruption.[29] How could we ever think ourselves capable of having a relationship with Holy God when we fall so far short of desiring his glory?

If this is the diagnosis, then what is the prognosis?

> Now we know that whatever the law says, it says to those who are
> under the law, that every mouth may be stopped, and all the world

28. Wells, *No Place for Truth*, 183.
29. Plantinga, *Breviary of Sin*, 31.

> may become guilty before God. Therefore by the deeds of the law
> no flesh will be justified in His sight, for by the law is the knowl-
> edge of sin. (vv. 19–20)

I think we miss the point of all this if we understand Paul to be saying that we are a bunch of dirty rotten people; that there is no hope for us
because we are so perverted and God just wants to send us to hell. Instead,
he is saying two incredibly significant things:

First, that at the very root of the human condition is an incapability
to live a God-centered life. We were created with that ability but we lost it
because of sin entering into the world.

In response, one might say, "Dave, are you talking about original sin?
I've never understood how God can consider us responsible for Adam and
Eve's sin." He doesn't; we are responsible for our own, but the very fact that
we can't be any different than Adam and Eve gives evidence of the fact that
we are born with this sinful condition. The ancient church used to say that
human nature was *despoiled* of its powers by original sin; it stripped away
the protective covering of who we were created to be in God's image and
turned us into beasts.

There is a disturbing portion of a book by Pierre van Paassan that I
would like to share with you. Let me set the scene: Nazi troops had captured a Jewish rabbi, stripped him naked, bent him over a barrel and beat
him with a leather strap, and crushed underfoot the false teeth that had
fallen out of the rabbi's mouth. Then they straightened him up and gathered
around him in a semi-circle. They took scissors and cut away the right side
of the rabbi's beard and the left side of the hair on his head; stepped back
and laughed. They ordered him to say something in Hebrew.

Slowly he said, "Thou shalt love the Lord thy God with all thy heart . . ."

Then one of them interrupted, "Were you not preparing your sermon
this morning?"

"Yes," said the rabbi.

"Well, preach it to us. You'll never again see your synagogue; we've just
burned it. Go ahead, preach the sermon . . . Quiet now, Jacob is going to
preach a sermon to us."

"Could I have my hat?" asked the rabbi.

"Can't you preach without a hat?" a soldier retorted.

"Give him his hat!" came the order. The sight of the naked man with a
hat on made them laugh all the more.

Then the rabbi spoke, "God created man in his image and likeness . . . That was to be my text for the coming Sabbath."[30]

This is why sin is so despicable because it defaces, corrupts, mocks—fallen from our original design to be able to do something like this to another human being created in God's image. This is also why when we stand before the throne of God in judgment, our mouth's will be silenced; no longer trying to justify our sinful behavior, but overwhelmed by the awareness of our sinful condition that has fallen so far short of God's glory!

The second thing that Paul says in verse 20 is that "no one will be declared righteous in God's sight by the works of the law." The reason: Doing good things cannot heal our spiritual condition—it may make us look good on the outside, like putting a tuxedo on a corpse, but it cannot make us alive to God.

Then why did God even bother to give us the law and those rules about how we should live? Look at the end of verse 20: "through the law we become conscious of our sin" (NIV). The law of God was given to reveal our sin, not to be our salvation. Paul gets into this in Romans 7; if we did not have the law, then we would never know our true condition and how much we have fallen short of God's glory. The law of God functions as a mirror to help us see our true need. Every morning I look into the mirror to see my need of a shave. Just as I would never take the mirror off the wall and use it to shave with, so the law is not an instrument by which we can be saved.

Donald Grey Barnhouse, for many years the pastor of Tenth Presbyterian Church in Philadelphia, developed a diagnostic question that would help him know how to deal with the many people who used to come to him. He would want to know if they believed in Christ or not, so he would ask them this: "If you were to die this very minute and stand before the throne of God, how would you answer if God asked you, 'What right do you have to come into my heaven?'" He found that all the responses fell into one of three general categories:

1. "Look at my record." Right there is the problem. Our record will not get us into heaven but is what will keep us out.

2. "Nothing to say." This is the more appropriate response, because when we stand in God's presence and our lives are made transparent in the

---

30. van Paassan, *That Day Alone*, 310–12.

light of his holy presence, we will not open our mouths in our own defense.

3. "In Christ alone." I wrote the following poem: "This will be my only plea, the fact that Jesus died for me. His blood and righteousness alone will merit my eternal home. If I had trusted something less, I'd be cursed instead of blessed."

So . . .

> Come you weary, heavy laden—lost and ruined by the fall.
> If you tarry till you're better, you will never come at all.
> —Joseph Hart

IV

Right Standing with God Given By God Through Jesus Christ (3:21—5:21)

PROVIDED BY FAITH (3:21-31)

Review

THE SCRIPTURE HAS REVEALED our sinful condition. Not all of us are adulterers, felons, drunkards, or whatever else you might consider perverse and depraved. Some of us are more bent than others of us. The issue, however, is that all of us have fallen short of God's glory and none of us is righteous. Such unrighteousness is inexcusable and we will be silent in view of God's final judgment because no one will be declared righteous by observing the law. The reference to observing the law, I believe, is referring to the meritorious works of righteousness done by the Jews in order to gain salvation. I do not hold to the "new perspective on Paul" advanced by E. P. Sanders. This view states that Palestinian Judaism was not a religion of amassing merit by keeping the law ("good works"), but rather that pattern of obedience which served as "boundary markers" or "badges of the covenant," circumcision, Sabbath observance, and dietary laws which distinguished the Jew from the gentile world and preserved their status as the people of the covenant. Thus, according to this perspective, Paul's concern was not setting forth an individual's pathway to finding peace with God, as much as attacking the barrier of ethnic separation between Jew and gentile due to the boundary markers of the law.[1]

Preview

Paul's classic "But now" introduces an incredible way by which God has broken into the darkness of human depravity and has made known a way of right-standing with God apart from observing the law. This way, which was foreshadowed in the Law and the Prophets (Scripture), has come to us through faith alone in the completed work of Jesus Christ alone. Thus, in spite of falling short of God's glory, we are justified freely through the marvelous grace of God.

> But now the righteousness of God apart from the law is revealed, being witnessed to by the Law and the Prophets, even the righteousness of God, through faith in Jesus Christ, to all who believe. For there is no difference; for all have sinned and fall short of the glory of God, being justified freely by His grace through the redemption that is in Christ Jesus. (vv. 21–25)

Perhaps there are those who believe that their difficulties in life demand a real solution and not some vague theological truth. However, Paul is unapologetically convinced and is unashamed that the truth of the gospel spoken here is at the core of whatever we face. At the basis of everything with which we struggle, it is imperative to know and experience that we are "in the right" with God; that we are not under his condemnation but have been made the recipients of his grace and forgiveness through faith in Jesus Christ. The Buddha found his answer to life's struggle by developing detachment from all things and escaping into "nothingness" through enlightenment—all of this without any dependency on the divine. Paul's answer is found by facing life's suffering head-on by attaching oneself to Jesus Christ by faith.

1. For a critique of the 'new perspective," see J. D. G. Dunn's article in Donfried, *Romans Debate*, 299–308; also, chapter 8 of *Adam, Christ, and Covenant* by A. T. B. McGowen.

Notice, first of all, that this righteousness of God is not his judging-righteousness, but his saving-righteousness.[2] The law reveals and condemns the sin of Jew and gentile—it cannot save. Only the righteousness that God can give can save both Jew and gentile when received "through faith in Jesus Christ." Thus, the opposite of condemnation is justification.[3] Justification by faith is a legal declaration of righteousness pronounced by God over the sinner who believes in the death and resurrection of Jesus Christ on his/her behalf. It is a gracious gift, a bestowal, an imputing (crediting) of a righteous status.

Martin Luther insisted that this is a righteousness that is *extra nos* (apart from us). He also called it an *iustitiam alienum* (alien righteousness). The Roman Church rejected Luther's perspective on justification by faith by calling it "a legal fiction." They believed that justification takes place at baptism and that it includes being infused with supernatural righteousness. They would ask: "How could God declare someone righteous who was not truly righteous?" But Luther claimed that the Bible maintained the idea of *simil iustus et peccator* (at the same time righteous and still a sinner). This means that justification is the justification of the ungodly, who, though already justified by the imputation of Christ's righteousness, are still ungodly to the extent that sin remains in them. The good news is that we do not have to wait until we are inherently righteous before God reckons or counts us as just, remits our sins, or adopts us into his family.[4]

Secondly, right-standing with God through faith and not through meritorious works "has been made known in the Law and the Prophets." It is not a new innovation but something that has been (perfect tense) made known. What was there in the Law that could possibly have contained this righteousness by faith? Perhaps this is a reference to the entire sacrificial system of the Old Testament which, though but a shadow of the good things to come (Heb 10:1), was nonetheless based upon the grace and mercy of God. It might also be a reference to Psalm 32:1 and 2, which Paul will mention in the next chapter when he speaks of Abraham and justification by faith: "Blessed is he whose transgressions are forgiven, whose sins are covered. Blessed is the man whose sin the Lord does not count against him and in his spirit is found no deceit." And what in the Prophets may

2. Schreiner, *Romans*, 181.

3. Stott, *Romans*, 110.

4. Sproul, *Faith Alone*, 25.

have pointed to this right-standing with God through the death of another? Perhaps the reference is to Isaiah 53:4–6:

> Surely he took up our infirmities and carried our sorrows, yet we considered him stricken by God, smitten by him, and afflicted. But he was pierced for our transgressions, he was crushed for our iniquities; the punishment that brought us peace was upon him, and by his wounds we are healed. We all, like sheep, have gone astray, each of us has turned to his own way; and the LORD has laid on him the iniquity of us all. (NIV)

Paul continues:

> whom God set forth as a propitiation by His blood, though faith, to demonstrate His righteousness, because in His forbearance God had passed over the sins that were previously committed, to demonstrate at the present time His righteousness, that He might be just and the justifier of the one who has faith in Jesus. (vv. 25–26)

Thus, the source of our justification is the grace of God, the ground of our justification is Christ's work on the cross, and the means of our justification is faith in Christ. The NIV translates the word *hilasterion* as "a sacrifice of atonement" (expiation). I believe the word is best understood as "propitiation" (the act of satisfying, or appeasing). C. H. Dodd, N. H. Young, and others reject this concept of propitiation as inappropriate; to think that God's anger had to be appeased and therefore Jesus sacrificed himself for us.

However, Paul clearly states that it was God who presented Christ to be our salvation, and that his death satisfies the justice, which a Holy God demands. It answers the question, "How can a Holy God let sinners off the hook by the death of another?" John Stott asks a similar question and then answers it: "How then could God express simultaneously his holiness in judgment and his love in pardon? Only by providing a divine substitute for the sinner, so that the substitute would receive the judgment and the sinner the pardon."[5] So God takes the sinner off the hook by putting Jesus on the hook. Thus Paul's point; this is how God can "be just and the justifier of the one who believes in Jesus."

What about Paul's next statement that Christ's death vindicated God's justice? "Because in His forbearance God had passed over the sins that were previously committed, to demonstrate at the present time His righteousness." The writer of Hebrews acknowledges that it was "impossible for the

5. Stott, *Romans*, 111.

blood of bulls and goats to take away sin" (Heb 10:4). And also that "sacrifices and offerings, burnt offerings and sin offerings you did not desire, nor were you pleased with them—although the law required them to be made" (Heb 10:8). The sacrificial system had no efficacy to forgive sin or to save; it only foreshadowed the forgiveness that was to come in Jesus Christ. Thus forbearance (*paresis*), *passing over* or *letting go unpunished*, was not justification because justification requires propitiation which animal sacrifices never accomplished.

In Acts 14:16 and 17:30 Paul also mentions God's forbearance in relationship to the nations. Referring to the past generations, he says that God "allowed the nations to walk in their own ways and overlooked their ignorance." Such forbearance on the part of God "was liable to be interpreted as indifference to the claims of justice and suspension of judgment as revocation and remission of the same."[6] However, the Bible teaches that God's tolerance and patience was not only to lead to repentance (Rom 2:4; 2 Pet 3:9), but was also exercised in looking ahead to the final sacrifice of Christ. Paul clearly states that this shows God to be just as well as merciful; he is just and the justifier. By this statement, Paul also implies that those who look to the law to save or to forgive are looking to something which does not have the power to do either. It also shows that justification is impossible without the cross.

> The forgiveness accomplished through the cross is the costly forgiveness worthy of God . . . since it involves nothing less than God's bearing the intolerable burden of that evil himself in the person of his own dear Son. . . . [It is] the disclosure of the fullness of God's hatred of man's evil [while] at the same time . . . it is real and complete forgiveness.[7]
>
> Where is boasting then? It is excluded. By what law? Of works? No, but by the law of faith. Therefore we conclude that a man is]justified by faith apart from the deeds of the law. Or is He the God of the Jews only? Is He not also the God of the Gentiles? Yes, of the Gentiles also, since there is one God who will justify the circumcised by faith and the uncircumcised through faith. Do we then make void the law through faith? Certainly not! On the contrary, we establish the law. (vv. 27–31)

6. Murray, *Romans*, 119.
7. Cranfield, *Romans*, 75.

Boasting of one's personal righteousness as well as the privileges of being an ethnic Jew was once the characteristic of Paul's life: "circumcised on the eighth day, of the people of Israel, of the tribe of Benjamin, a Hebrew of the Hebrews; in regards to the law a Pharisee . . . as to legalistic righteousness, faultless" (Phil 3:4–6, NIV). Where is such boasting now? It is excluded (*ekkleio*, "shut out"). It is interesting that Paul uses the same word in Galatians 4:17 of the Judaizers who wished to shut out the Galatian Christians from the true gospel. With the same jarring clarity, Paul says that the self-congratulatory nature of works-righteousness is completely excluded by the principle of faith, all because of God's grace in Jesus Christ—"and that not of yourselves, it is a gift of God; not by works, so that no one can boast" (Eph 2:8–9, NIV). "Therefore, may I never boast except in the cross of our Lord Jesus Christ" (Gal 6:14, NIV).

Since our right standing with God is all about faith and not about culture, race, or privilege, then God is the God of gentile as well as Jew. "The message is simple: all who believe in Jesus belong to the same family and should be eating at the same table. That is what Paul's doctrine of justification is all about."[8]

Paul asks a final question which he will more completely answer in Romans 6–8: "Do we, then, make void the law through faith?" There may also be something else that Paul is here anticipating from his critics. Is the whole Torah (Mosaic dispensation) obviated by the principle of faith? Does the law have any value at all to the believer? He will answer that specifically in Romans 7, but for now he responds by the simple affirmation, "Certainly not! On the contrary, we establish the law." Justification by faith does not render the law useless; rather, it is established (*histemi*, "has abiding value"). However, he has more to say about justification by faith before he gives us a fuller explanation of this simple affirmation. One needs to exercise patience with Paul.

B. PROVEN BY THE EXAMPLE OF ABRAHAM (4:1–25)

Review

Paul has argued that the whole world is guilty before God and under his wrath. God's wrath is not so much that he loses his temper or flies into a

---

8. Wright, *New Tasks*, 168.

rage when he sees sin. Rather, God's wrath is his holy abhorrence to sin due to his perfectly righteous character. Escape from this wrath will not come from any human source or else it would have happened by now. No one can make himself acceptable to God by applying human solutions. Even our attempts at justice and religious zeal are ultimately destructive—look at the Middle East. The good news is that God has taken the initiative to provide a way of escaping his own wrath. That way is through faith in Jesus Christ who has satisfied God's justice against sin, taken away the wrath of God, and provided forgiveness of sins through his death and resurrection. All who believe in Christ are righteous ("in the right") before God; they are justified through faith in Christ.

Preview

Paul moves on to illustrate the points he has just made. The main character of this chapter is Abraham. Who better? Jew and gentile held him in honor. Even today, he is deeply respected by Jew, Christian, and Muslim. If Paul could show that this concept of justification by faith was true for Abraham, then he would have significantly proven his point to those who doubted him. N. T. Wright also suggests that Abraham is used by Paul as more than just an example of justification. "He (Paul) sees God's promise to Abraham as a single-plan-through-Israel-for-the-world; in short, the covenant. Abraham is where it all starts."[9]

The one major point that Paul makes in this entire chapter, which we see right from the start: Abraham was justified by faith and not by human achievement (4:1–8).

> What then shall we say was gained by Abraham, our forefather according to the flesh? For if Abraham was justified by works, he has something to boast about, but not before God. For what does the Scripture say? "Abraham believed God, and it was counted to him as righteousness." Now to the one who works, his wages are not counted as a gift but as his due. And to the one who does not work but believes in him who justifies the ungodly, his faith is counted as righteousness, just as David also speaks of the blessing of the one to whom God counts righteousness apart from works: "Blessed are those whose lawless deeds are forgiven, and whose

9. Wright, *Justification*, 216–217.

sins are covered; blessed is the man against whom the Lord will not count his sin." (ESV)

Did you hear (see) a word repeated five times in this section, and eleven times in the entire chapter? The word "counted," also translated "accounted," "credited," "reckoned," "imputed." It is from the Greek *logizomai*, which is a word taken from the business world. It means a reckoning or crediting (imputing) of payment: "Now to the one who works, his wages are not counted as a gift but as his due" (v. 4). Imagine a situation where you put in a tough forty-hour week plus ten hours overtime. Your boss comes to you, hands you your check and says, "Here's a little gift for you for all the work you did this week." What would you say? "Hey, boss, if you want to give me a turkey on Thanksgiving as a gift, that's fine, but don't call this check a gift. I worked my tail off for it and I earned every penny!" You told him, didn't you?

However, imagine a situation where you are convalescing at home after using up all your sick time, personal time, vacation time, and you are waiting for your disability insurance to kick in. Your boss visits you with a check for forty hours plus ten hours overtime. You say, "But I didn't work for it!" He replies, "That's okay, I'm accounting it to you as a gift." Where's your boasting now? What is there to boast about except the grace of your employer? It would be a bit humbling, wouldn't it?

Paul applies such a scenario to Abraham when he quotes Genesis 15:6: "Abraham believed God and it was counted to him as righteousness." When Abraham worried about the fact that he and his wife were childless, God promised that he and Sarah would have offspring too numerous to count—comparable to the stars in the sky. Abraham looked at his seventy-five-year-old body and his sixty-five-year-old wife and thought, "You've got to be kidding." He knew they were in no position to bring about this promise in their own strength, so he trusted that God would accomplish what was impossible for him. In response, God credited right-standing (righteousness) to Abraham, not because he earned it, but simply because he believed God's promise about a son. And Paul in Galatians 3:16 interprets this is as a promise of a future Son, Jesus Christ, thus demonstrating that Abraham's faith (and all who share Abraham's faith) was a saving faith.

It is interesting that the accepted Jewish understanding of this verse is that Abraham was justified because of his *faithfulness*, not his faith. Also in Roman Catholic theology there is the concept of *condign merit* by which a person who believes in Christ receives a reward for works that God finds worthy. You can see how such interpretations would change the concept of righteousness from a gift to a wage. But Paul reiterates (v. 5) that God justifies the "ungodly" (Rom 5:6), not through faithfulness or works of human performance, but through faith. This may have greatly disturbed the Jewish world to hear Abraham called ungodly, but understand that Abraham was a Mesopotamian moon-worshipper before he became a believer. And God made his covenant with Abraham after he had believed.

This is the point Paul makes in 4:9–15, that Abraham was declared righteous fourteen years before he received the covenant sign of circumcision. Paul is not merely describing how we are put right with God, but how we become part of the family of Abraham. Thus Abraham is not only the father of the Jewish nation but he is the father of everyone (Jew and gentile) who is justified by faith in Jesus Christ. Circumcision had nothing to do with Abraham's justification, but its significance was as a sign and seal of his faith—much like baptism is in the New Testament. In the same way, Paul says that the very promise upon which his justifying faith was based came 430 years before the giving of the law. (Galatians 3:6–25 is an excellent commentary on the whole of Romans 4.)

> Is this blessing then only for the circumcised, or also for the un-
> circumcised? For we say that faith was counted to Abraham as
> righteousness. How then was it counted to him? Was it before
> or after he had been circumcised? It was not after, but before he
> was circumcised. He received the sign of circumcision as a seal
> of the righteousness that he had by faith while he was still un-
> circumcised. The purpose was to make him the father of all who
> believe without being circumcised, so that righteousness would
> be counted to them as well, and to make him the father of the
> circumcised who are not merely circumcised but who also walk
> in the footsteps of the faith that our father Abraham had before he
> was circumcised. For the promise to Abraham and his offspring
> that he would be heir of the world did not come through the law
> but through the righteousness of faith. For if it is the adherents
> of the law who are to be the heirs, faith is null and the promise is
> void. For the law brings wrath, but where there is no law there is
> no transgression. (vv. 9–15, ESV)

The first application that Paul makes in verses 18–22 is that God accounts to us a relational right-standing with himself apart from human performance because we are impotent to save ourselves.

> In hope he believed against hope, that he should become the father of many nations, as he had been told, "So shall your offspring be." He did not weaken in faith when he considered his own body, which was as good as dead (since he was about a hundred years old), or when he considered the barrenness of Sarah's womb. No unbelief made him waver concerning the promise of God, but he grew strong in his faith as he gave glory to God, fully convinced that God was able to do what he had promised. That is why his faith was "counted to him as righteousness." (ESV)

We are as impotent as Abraham to make ourselves right with God. As an old hymn writer once put it, "Not what these hands have done can save this guilty soul; not what this toiling flesh has borne can make my spirit whole. Not what I feel or do can give me peace with God; not all my prayers and sighs and tears can bear my awful load."[10]

It is only as God himself gives us right standing by his grace that we can have a relationship with him.

> Man . . . is a castaway in a state of wrath, and is bound hand and foot, so that he cannot lay hold of the cords of love thrown out to him in the Gospel. The most skilled craftsman cannot work without tools; neither can the most skillful musician play well on an instrument that is out of tune. How can anyone believe, or repent, whose understanding is darkness and whose heart is stony? The arms of natural abilities are too short to reach supernatural help.[11]

The second application Paul makes is that God counts righteousness to us through faith: "But the words 'it was counted to him' were not written for his [Abraham's] sake alone, but for ours also. It will be counted to us who believe in him who raised from the dead Jesus our Lord, who was delivered up for our trespasses and raised for our justification" (vv. 23–25, ESV).

Faith is not a reward that merits righteousness. We are never saved on account of our faith, but always through faith; an instrumental means through which God graciously applies his righteousness to us. "Faith is not an alternative to righteousness, but a means by which we are declared righteous."[12]

During the Reformation, the argument was not over whether faith was necessary for justification. Both Protestants and Roman Catholics

---

10. Bonar, "Not What These Hands Have Done."

11. Boston, *Human Nature*, 191.

12. Stott, *Romans*, 126.

agreed, and still do agree, that faith is required for justification. The debate centered around the instrumental cause of justification: Is faith alone the instrument of justification or are works included as well? Romans 3:28 says it clearly: "For we hold that one is justified by faith apart from the works of the law. That which makes us right with God is faith alone, while works are an expression of our faith."

The final application that Paul makes is tucked away earlier in this chapter: God also refuses to count our sins against us. "Blessed are those whose lawless deeds are forgiven, and whose sins are covered; blessed is the man against whom the Lord will not count his sin" (vv. 7–8, ESV).

We are introduced to another top gun from the Old Testament in this section. Paul quotes King David who wrote Psalm 32, speaking of the great blessing of being reckoned as righteous in God's sight. It should be noted that David was a believer, one whom God had declared righteous and yet he committed adultery, and tried to cover it up by becoming a conspirator in the murder of an innocent man. He kept his crime to himself for about a year before the prophet Nathan confronted him. David confessed his sin and repented of what he had done and wrote Psalm 32, which Paul quotes in verses 7–8. (See also Ps 103:10–12.)

Justification by grace through faith involves two actions on the part of God on behalf of the believer: first, the crediting of righteousness to our account, though we are morally and spiritually bankrupt; secondly, the forgiveness of all of our sins and never counting them against us again. That is why the play on the word justified is so accurate: "just-as-if-I'd" never sinned. When a person believes in Christ, that person is counted righteous in the sight of God. Every sin—past, present, and future—is washed away and God will never bring up our sins again. The psalmist has said, "As far as the East is from the West, so far has He removed our sins from us" (Ps 103:12). The prophet Micah put it this way: "Who is a pardoning God like you, who pardons sin and forgives transgression. . . and hurls all our iniquities into the depths of the sea?" (Mic 7:18–20, NIV). God does not throw them into the shallow water where we can go and scoop them out again, but he casts our sin into the depths of the sea where they are lost forever in his grace.

As believers, our slate is clean with God because of Christ. This should not cause us to respond by sinning all the more because we know we are forgiven. As Paul said in the last chapter (3:27), all boasting is excluded on the basis of salvation by faith and not by our works. This truth should humble us and motivate us through gratitude to live in such a way as to never disappoint the one who has been so gracious. Our prayer should be: "O God, thank you for your mercy and I am awed by your grace and forgiveness, now that I stand completely accepted and loved in your sight. Now, help me by my love to show, just how much to you I owe. Amen."

However, the not-yet believer's sin is still on his shoulders instead of stapled to the cross, and s/he is under the wrath of God. If she were to die, she would spend an eternity alienated from God, just as she is now separated from him. There is nothing humanly or religiously possible to be done about this. The only alternative is to trust in what Jesus Christ has already done by his death and resurrection. One must respond in deep humility and faith. It matters not how strong or sincere one's faith, rather it is the reliability of the object in which that faith is placed. The sincerity of my faith will not keep me from falling on my backside if this chair in which I am sitting is flawed and collapses. Thus one can be sincere, but also be sincerely wrong.

If you have not yet received Christ, your prayer should be: "O God, be merciful to me a sinner! I am sorry for my rebellion against you and I know that I have accrued a debt too large to pay. Thank you that you have provided a way by which my sins can be forgiven and through which I can be put right with you. I accept the gift that you offer me and ask that Jesus Christ would come into my life by your Holy Spirit and justify me in your sight. Amen.

C. THE FRUIT OF JUSTIFICATION (5:1–11)

Review

Paul has argued that the whole world is guilty before God and under his wrath. He has also said that God has provided a way of escaping his own wrath by believing in the death and resurrection of Jesus Christ. The person who exercises such faith is justified in the sight of God and has the very righteousness of God given to him/her as a gift. Abraham is then presented as an example of justification by faith. Paul's main point in chapter 4 is to show that Abraham was justified by faith and not by the works of the law and, therefore, Jew and gentile must be rescued in the same way.

Preview

In this section, Paul now relates the effects of justification in the life of the believer. Since the principle of justification has been established and illustrated, the fruit of justification remains to be presented.

> Therefore, having been justified by faith, we have peace with God through our Lord Jesus Christ, through whom also we have access by faith into this grace in which we stand, and rejoice in hope of the glory of God. And not only that, but we also glory in tribulations, knowing that tribulation produces perseverance; and perseverance, character; and character, hope. Now hope does not disappoint, because the love of God has been poured out in our hearts by the Holy Spirit who was given to us. (vv. 1–5)

The first piece of fruit of justification in the life of the believer is that "we have peace with God through our Lord Jesus Christ." The picture that Paul paints of the sinner is not one who is merely poor, lost, and blind, but of one who is a rebel (Eph 2:1–3) who is at enmity with God. In fact, in verse 10 of this chapter, Paul describes God's great love for us being revealed by Christ's death while we were his unreconciled enemies. Since we have received his death and resurrection as ours through faith, there is no longer enmity, wrath, or condemnation coming from God—but peace. I once heard R. C. Sproul relate a story of playing stickball on the streets of Pittsburgh when he was a kid during World War II. One day, people suddenly came running out of their houses into the streets hugging and kissing each other, crying, "It's over, it's over!" His mother embraced him and cried, "The war is over and your father is coming home!" R. C. was so excited that there was finally peace, but he soon learned how temporary that peace was when just a few years later our country was fighting in Korea. However, the peace with God that comes to us through his justifying grace is everlasting. Truly "there is no condemnation to those who are in Christ Jesus" (Rom 8:1). "He makes wars to cease. . . . He breaks the bow and shatters the spear" (Ps 46:9, ESV).

The second fruit of justification is that through Christ "we have gained access by faith into this grace in which we now stand." Commentators disagree on whether the Greek word *prosagoge* should be translated "introduction" or "access." If the former, then the emphasis is on Christ bringing us near to God and instating us in his grace.[13] However, if it means the

---

13. Murray, *Romans*, 160.

latter, which I believe it does, it emphasizes the privilege of "drawing nigh to God" with free access—something the high priest of Israel could do only once a year! God shook the world at the death of Christ and the temple curtain was ripped in two. "Let us then with confidence draw near to the throne of grace, that we may receive mercy and find grace to help in time of need" (Heb 4:16, ESV).

We should not overlook that very important phrase "in which we stand." I want to draw a word picture for you so you will need to use your imagination. In your mind, draw a circle with a little opening on one side with a cross just outside the opening. Now color everything outside of the circle (including the cross) the color of *wrath*—whatever color you think that is. Now color everything inside the circle the color of *grace* and close up the little opening in the circle. One more thing—put a dot in the middle of the circle; that is you. Now, what happens if you sin? Do you fall out of the circle (remember the circle is closed) or do you fall somewhere within the circle because that is where you are already standing?

Justification positions us in the circle of God's grace and even when we sin, we do not fall out of grace, but we fall back into it. Our confession and repentance take place within the circle of God's grace because it is there Christ has positioned us. Our relationship with God will never again be broken. Never again will we face the wrath of God because peace has been declared. We have been brought into God's very family and we are standing in his grace. I cannot emphasize enough how much you must be convinced of this. You must believe that you are standing in the assurance of God's grace or else you will never get on with the process of growing in that grace.

The third fruit or effect of our justification is oriented towards the future. *And we rejoice in the hope of the glory of God.* The concept of the glory of God is massive and beyond the scope of our discussion here. However, suffice it say that not only is the glory of God God's ultimate concern, but everything that God does is for the purpose of his own glory. We who were created in his image and likeness were created for his glory as are the sun, moon, and stars (Ps 19:1). Creation was marred because of the fall and God's image in humankind defaced. However, everyone that God has called by his Name has been created for his glory (Isa 43:7; Jer 13:11); we have been chosen in Christ to the praise of his glory (Eph 1:6); someday God's glory will be revealed completely at the consummation of his eternal purposes in Christ, and every eye will see and every tongue confess that Jesus is Lord to the glory of God the Father (Phil 2:11); and someday God's glory will be revealed in us, and in creation itself, which has been groaning because of the fall (Rom 8:18–21). Someday the earth will be "filled with the knowledge of the glory of the Lord as the waters cover the sea" (Hab 2:14). Just as the fruit of justification affect our past (peace with God), and our present (access to God), so they will affect our future. Thus we rejoice in the hope of God's glory.

What incredible blessings have come to us through our justification! However, Paul sounds a very realistic note when he presents the fourth fruit: "we also rejoice in our sufferings." These sufferings (*thlipsis*) refer specifically to the pressures and opposition that Christians receive from a world that hates the gospel. The word is often translated "tribulations" or "afflictions" and is mentioned by Paul in such passages as Romans 8:35–39, 1 Corinthians 4:9–13, 2 Corinthians 1:4–10, 11:23–30, and 12:7–10. Rather than eliciting self-pity from Paul, these afflictions actually cause him to rejoice because they accomplish a developmental work in his life and character. Reminiscent of a similar cadenza in James 1, Paul acknowledges that his sufferings accomplish a steadfast endurance and not a willowy faith; this endurance produces character that has been refined through testing; and this proven character produces a hope that is firmly reliant upon God and his promises. John Murray suggests that these qualities can be diagrammed in the shape of a circle; beginning with the hope of God's glory and ending in the hope of God's glory. "We glory in tribulations because they have an eschatological orientation—they subserve the interests of hope."[14]

Paul then makes a statement that just explodes with meaning when properly understood. Suffering not only produces all of the qualities just mentioned culminating in hope, but it also becomes the context in which we experience the superabundance of God's love for us. "And hope does not put us to shame, because God's love has been poured out into our hearts through the Holy Spirit, who has been given to us." Paul could be speaking here of God's love for us and our love for God. Like a "cloudburst on a parched countryside, what the Holy Spirit does is to make us deeply and refreshingly aware that God loves us."[15] And this "poured out love" becomes the very source of our love for God, which has an expulsive power to push away our love for the world. Thomas Chalmers (1780–1847), a minister in the Church of Scotland, wrote a discourse on the text of 1 John 2:15, "Love not the world or the things that are in the world. If any man loves the world, the love of the Father is not in him." The title of his discourse

14. Murray, *Romans*, 164.
15. Stott, *Romans*, 143.

was *The Expulsive Power of a New Affection*. His basic premise was: "It is . . . impossible . . . for the heart, by any innate elasticity of its own, to cast the world away from it; and thus reduce itself to a wilderness. . . . The only way to dispossess it of an old affection is by the expulsive power of a new one."[16]

And what is this new affection that has such expulsive power? Chalmers claims that it comes to us though a proper understanding of the gospel:

> It is God apprehended by the believer as God in Christ . . . when He stands dismantled of the terrors which belong to Him as an offended lawgiver and when we are enabled by faith, which is His own gift, to see His glory in the face of Jesus Christ, and to hear His beseeching voice, as it protests good will to men, and entreats the return of all who will to a full pardon and gracious acceptance. It is then, that a love paramount to the love of the world, and at length expulsive of it, first arises in the regenerated bosom.[17]

This fruit of justification is not a special experience in the Holy Spirit found by just a few. It is available to all who cry out to their God in the midst of affliction and who find special grace and mercy in time of need. However, tribulation is not the only time in which God demonstrates his love for us. It has also been proven in a more objective way by Christ's death on the cross. Paul expands on this topic in a magnificent way in verses 6–11:

> For when we were still without strength, in due time Christ died for the ungodly. For scarcely for a righteous man will one die; yet perhaps for a good man someone would even dare to die. But God demonstrates His own love toward us, in that while we were still sinners, Christ died for us. Much more then, having now been justified by His blood, we shall be saved from wrath through Him. For if when we were enemies we were reconciled to God through the death of His Son, much more, having been reconciled, we shall be saved by His life. And not only that, but we also rejoice in God through our Lord Jesus Christ, through whom we have now received the reconciliation.

The grandeur of God's love for us is found in the costliness of the gift, his own dear Son, in contrast with our utter unworthiness. While it is scarcely possible that someone would give his life for a good and righteous person worthy of love and respect, it is utterly inconceivable that anyone would die for a scoundrel. And yet Christ died for us—while we were

16. Chalmers, *Expulsive Power*, 10.
17. Chalmers, *Expulsive Power*, 17.

powerless, while we were ungodly, while we were still sinners, and while we were enemies. As with Charles Wesley, we respond "Amazing love, how can it be, that Thou my God shouldst die for me!"[18]

Such love also forms the basis of the assurance of our salvation. Here Paul uses what theologians call *a fortiori arguments*—that if one thing is true, *how much more* must something else be true. If we have been justified by Christ's blood, by which we have obtained all the blessings of justification, *how much more* will we be saved from God's wrath through him. If we are reconciled to God through Christ's death because of his great love for us, *how much more* will we be saved by the life of Christ. "There is therefore now no condemnation to those who are in Christ Jesus" (Rom 8:1). In this we presently rejoice because the wrath of God has been satisfied, the fear of God has been eliminated, and the love of God for us in Christ has given us a secured hope.

D. THE OBEDIENCE OF CHRIST AND OUR NEW IDENTITY IN HIM (5:12–21)

Review

We have seen Paul demonstrate God's justifying grace in Christ against the background of the universal extent of human guilt. We have also seen the application of this guilt to both Jew and gentile as well as that of equal access to the grace of God. All are children of Abraham by faith in Jesus' death and resurrection and will fully experience the fruit of their justification.

Preview

At first glance, this section may seem like an annoying intrusion into the stream of Paul's thought. However, the *dia touto* (therefore, for this reason) indicates a relationship with what has come before[19] and a link to what will follow in chapter 6.[20] The reconciliatory power of Christ (5:11) has done nothing less than to inaugurate a new humanity (5:12–21) eventuating in a new creation (8:18–25). Thus, in this section, Paul compares and contrasts

18. Wesley, "And Can It Be."
19. Schreiner, *Romans*, 271.
20. Stott, *Romans*, 148.

the old humanity (in Adam) with the new humanity (in Christ). Schreiner sees the theme of this section as hope. Dunn claims it portrays the universality of justification by faith. Cranfield sees it as a portrayal of the universal work of reconciliation.

As we examine the framework of the passage, it should be noted that Paul begins his main argument in verse 12, but immediately breaks off into a digression, verses 13–17, which is put in parentheses in most Bibles. Then he picks up his original thought in verse 18 and completes it in verse 21. We will follow his main thought here. If you grasp Paul's main idea, you can easily go back and understand his digression.

> Therefore, just as through one man sin entered the world, and death through sin, and thus death spread to all men, because all sinned . . . Therefore, as through one man's offense judgment came to all men, resulting in condemnation, even so through one Man's righteous act the free gift came to all men, resulting in justification of life. For as by one man's disobedience many were made sinners, so also by one Man's obedience many will be made righteous. Moreover the law entered that the offense might abound. But where sin abounded, grace abounded much more, so that as sin reigned in death, even so grace might reign through righteousness to eternal life through Jesus Christ our Lord.

Verse 12a

Death is not natural but came into the world as the direct result of one man's sin (Adam). In Genesis 2, God said to Adam, "You must not eat from the tree of the knowledge of good and evil, for when you eat of it you shall surely die" (NIV). Adam and Eve disobeyed the command of God but they did not immediately die. They lived for long time. However, some things did happen immediately: they hid from God because they were ashamed; God kicked them out of his presence, represented by the Garden of Eden. And so we understand from this that death is not only a physical event but also a relational and spiritual condition, evidenced by alienation and separation from God. Therefore, Paul teaches that death (physical and spiritual) was introduced into the world because of the sin of Adam. It was not part of God's original creation but an ugly intrusion into a good world. Not only do we physically die, but we are also alienated and separated from God even as we live. And so, this dual condition of death came into the world as the result of the sin of one man, Adam.

Verse 12b

Death spread to all humanity because all have sinned. How are we to understand this? Do we sin because we are sinners or are we sinners because we sin? Have we somehow participated in the sin of Adam and become sinners even before we were born, or is it that we have followed the example of Adam and sinned in our own persons, thereby becoming sinners? The first suggestion that we sin because we are sinners is really the doctrine of original sin introduced by Saint Augustine as he hammered out his biblical theology against Pelagius, a fifth-century monk. Pelagius held to the second suggestion and believed that Adam was just a bad example, which we followed and became sinners because of our own sin; that everyone starts off like Adam and freely chooses to corrupt himself. While we may like the second view because it sounds more American ("I'll do my own sinning, thank you!"), the first view is more in keeping with the force of the text. Death came to us because of the sin of Adam (v. 15), "through one man sin entered the world, and death through sin, and thus death spread to all men." At the same time, Paul says that we all have sinned. How do we understand this? Thomas Schreiner says that "original death" may be a more accurate term than "original sin":

> As a result of Adam's sin death entered the world and engulfed all people; all people enter the world alienated from God and spiritually dead by virtue of Adam's sin. [Also], by virtue of entering the world in the state of death (separated from God), all human beings sin."[21]

Verses 18–19

Jesus Christ is the representative head of a new humanity. Here we have a very clear picture that Paul is speaking about two representative men, Adam and Christ. (See also 1 Corinthians 15:45–49.) We are sinners by virtue of our corporate identity with Adam as the head of the human race. Sin is imputed or placed on the account of all of Adam's descendants. But now there is a new humanity, one headed by another representative man—Jesus

21. Schreiner, *Romans*, 276.

Christ. We become righteous by virtue of our corporate identity with him. Right-standing with God is imputed to all who are Christ's spiritual descendants. We are not used to thinking in terms of group solidarity because of our own culture's emphasis upon individuality. But in the culture of the Bible, people identified themselves as members of a family, tribe, or nation. Wars were decided by a battle of champions. Tribes were punished because of the sin of one person. Promises made to one generation were honored among future generations. So in the grand scheme of things, Paul sees Adam and Christ as not only historical figures but also as representative heads of two humanities. Douglas Moo addresses it this way:

> The perspective is corporate rather than individual. All people, Paul teaches, stand in relationship to one of two men, whose actions determine the eternal destiny of all who belong to them. Either one 'belongs to' Adam and is under the sentence of death because of his [Adam] sin, or disobedience, or one belongs to Christ and is assured of eternal life because of his [Christ] "righteous" act, or obedience.[22]

I have on my desk a souvenir that I picked up my last time in Moscow—a Matryoshka doll. It is a series of smaller dolls within a larger doll. Let's say that the smallest doll is you. You are neatly tucked away inside your parents, they are inside their parents, and so on. Whatever happens to your great, great, great, great grandparents will have an impact on you. Where they are born, who they marry, a genetic disorder, an addiction, a death—all of these will affect you, although you would never know it unless you did some genealogical research.

Paul is giving us a kind of genealogical perspective on our human family history. He simplifies it by saying there are only two families, Adam and Christ—either you are from one or the other. If you are in Adam, whatever happened to him happened to you. If you are in Christ, the same is true.

In verse 19, Paul makes the comparison between the disobedience of Adam and the obedience of Christ, and the consequences of these acts upon all humanity. He says that "through the disobedience of the one man the many were made [*kathistanai*, "appointed," "constituted"] sinners, so through the obedience of the one man the many will be made righteous." If our heritage is in Adam, this is what we reap because of his disobedience: death (relational, spiritual, and physical), condemnation, and domination by sin. If we are in Christ, this is our heritage due to his obedience: eternal life,

22. Moo, *Epistle to the Romans*, 315.

right-standing with God, and dominated by the superabundance of grace. A. T. B. McGowan calls this "Headship Theology" and describes it this way:

> God entered into a relationship with Adam in Genesis 2. In this relationship, Adam is viewed as the representative head of the human race such that his obedience or disobedience would affect all those whom he represented, namely, all humanity yet unborn. . . . Through his act of disobedience, judgment came upon the whole human race. The focus then turns to Christ. Out of his great love, God sent his Son to be a "second Adam." The second Adam represented all those who will ultimately be saved . . . Where Adam failed, Christ succeeded; where Adam disobeyed, Christ obeyed. Finally Christ offered himself up on the cross as an atoning sacrifice for sins, this is to be understood in terms of a penal substitution. By his one act of righteousness, Christ obtained salvation for all who are "in him."[23]

Verses 20–21

Christ's act of obedience brought eternal life and righteousness to all who believe in Him. It is important to note the language that Paul uses when he talks about the work of Christ and the grace of God. He uses superlatives like "abound," "abundance," "overflowing," "surpassing," how much more." All of these indicate that there is a radical dissimilarity between the consequences of Adam's disobedience and the obedience of Christ. Paul's language also shows the vast superiority of grace over sin in producing righteous living instead of death. As we will see in the next chapter, sin is a powerful force which reigns, rules, and enslaves those who are in Adam. But here we see that grace has invaded the world through Jesus Christ and is more powerful than sin and death. This grace has conquered sin so that we are no longer condemned before God but stand righteous before him. This grace also produces in us a changed life, which brings with it the gift of eternal life and means that death itself has been conquered. This gift of life is offered to anyone who believes in Jesus Christ—"to as many as received Him, to them He gave the right to be called the children of God" (John 1:12).

The question remains: To which humanity do I belong? I am either in Christ or in Adam.

---

23. McGowan, *Adam, Christ, and Covenant*, 127.

V

Grace-Based, Not Performance-Based Relationship with God (6–8)

A. THE REIGN OF SIN BROKEN BY OUR DEATH IN CHRIST, SYMBOLIZED BY BAPTISM (6:1–14)

Review

HAVING ESTABLISHED THE PRINCIPLE of justification by faith, by which God declares the sinner righteous through faith in Christ's work on the cross, Paul proceeded to show how such faith has changed our identity from being in Adam to being *in Christ* (an expression which Paul uses over 160 times in his letters). As we will see, it is this new identity that is gained for us by our justification and forms the basis of our sanctification, our growth in holiness.

Preview

In Romans 6, Paul's focus moves from justification (Christ's work *for* us) to sanctification (Christ's work *in* us). Please notice that these are not so much separate events, but one flows out of the other (sanctification flows out of justification). Having said this, it should be emphasized that they are not one in the same but distinctive works of God in the believer's life. (Remember that Roman Catholic theology sees them as the same.)

Paul is anticipating the objection that justification will cause one to disregard God's law. After all, he did say "for where sin increased, grace increased all the more" (Rom 5:20). We will see that Paul answers this objection twice; in verses 1–14 and then again in verses 15–23.

Verse 1

"Shall we go on sinning so that grace may increase?" (NIV). If God pours out his justifying grace more abundantly where sin is the greatest, why not keep on sinning greatly so that God's grace can be brought into sharper relief?

Verse 2

"By no means! We died to sin, how can we live in it any longer? (NIV). Paul doesn't argue for the impossibility of sin in the believer but the incongruity of it. Justification is not merely the imputing of Christ's righteousness to our accounts, but something happens to us as well. What? We die to sin.

Verses 3–5

"Or don't you know that all of us who were baptized into Christ Jesus were baptized into His death? We were therefore buried with Him through baptism into death in order that just as Christ was raised from the dead through the glory of the Father, we too may live a new life. If we have been united with Him like this in His death, we shall certainly also be united with Him in His resurrection" (NIV).

Water baptism is not merely a sign and seal of our faith in Jesus Christ; it is more, according to Paul. It is a linking together of my personal history with that of Christ's personal history. Note the linking phrases: "baptized into Christ . . . baptized into His death. . .buried with Him . . . united with Him in His death . . . united with Him in His resurrection." At baptism, the believer is baptized into the Name of Jesus. He/she receives a new identity. Our history, solidarity with Adam (old self), has been replaced by a new solidarity with Christ. Thus, from God's perspective, whatever happened to Christ has happened to us, and whatever will happen to Christ will also happen to us. For example, if I slip a piece of paper into a book I am holding, and close the book, whatever I then do with the book I also do with the paper. If Christ is the book and I am the paper in the book, then whatever happens to Christ happens to me. Christ is my new identity. His history is my history and his future is mine as well.

Verses 6–10

"For we know that our old self [Adam solidarity] was crucified with Him so that the body of sin might be done away with, that we should no longer be slaves to sin—because anyone who has died is freed from sin. Now if we died with Christ, we believe that we shall also live with Him. For we know that since Christ was raised from the dead, he cannot die again; death no longer has mastery over Him. The death He died, He died to sin once for all, but the life He lives, He lives to God" (NIV).

Paul states that my old self (old man, Adam solidarity), which was under the guilt, penalty, and dominion of death, was crucified in Christ when he died on the cross as my substitute. What was the effect? "That our body of sin might be done away with [*katargeo*, "defeated," "disabled," "deprived of power"] that we should no longer be slaves to sin." The "body of sin" does not mean that our bodies are sinful. Rather, it means that my old nature, which used my body to express itself (as an instrument), has now been deprived of its power to enslave and to turn my natural instincts into degraded passions. Now, because I am in Christ, I am free to use my body as an instrument of his righteousness. Sin's power to accuse and condemn has been broken. This is the significance of the phrase "freed from sin." The word *dedikaiotai* translates to "has been justified." Sin's power over the believer, while still influential, has been disabled and we are freed (justified) from its condemnation. (If Paul meant to say that we have been freed from sin's influence then he would have used the word *eleuthero*, which he does use in verses 18 and 22.)

Thus I disagree with commentators who interpret the concept of being "dead to sin" as being unresponsive to its impulses or free from its influence. Christ did not die so as to become unresponsive to sin but to pay its penalty and to break its condemning power, which is death. As Charles Wesley phrased it, "He breaks the power of cancelled sin and sets the prisoner free." And so, "Dead to sin as meaning dead to the influence and love of sin is entirely erroneous. Paul is not referring to a death to the power of sin but to a death to its guilt, that is, our justification."[1]

Verse 11

"Even so, consider (reckon, regard, look upon, count) yourselves dead to sin, but alive to God in Jesus Christ" (NIV). In other words, think about this very carefully: even though you don't feel dead to sin because some of the old software has been showing up on your new computer, you are to regard yourself as dead to its legal claims against you and are no longer under its authority. The key to holy living is found in the way you think rather than in how you feel. Christians "must revolt in the name of their rightful ruler, God, against sin's usurping rule."[2]

Verses 12–14

The conclusion to Paul's thought flows out of what he has already said. Therefore, since Christ died to sin and lives to God, and because we also died to sin and live to God in union with Christ, we should initiate the following:

- Refuse to let sin tyrannize us to obey its lusts.

- Stop presenting (present tense) our physical body as an instrument (*hoopla*, weapon) of unrighteousness.

- Present (aorist tense, indicating an act of commitment) yourself to God as the result of your new life and use your body as a weapon for righteousness.

Paul concludes with a powerful affirmation of this new management in verse 14: "For sin shall not be master over you, for you are not under law

1. Haldane, *Romans*, 251.
2. Cranfield, *Romans*, 316.

but under grace" (NIV). Is Paul saying, "For sin might not be your master" or "For sin need not be your master"? No! "For sin shall not be your master!" Why? Because "you are not under law but under grace." You are no longer under the jurisdiction of the law with its penalty and condemnation. Rather, you stand before God in an environment of pure grace because you are connected by faith to his Son and are justified.

Perhaps it will be hard to imagine the following scenario, but give it a try. You live in an efficiency apartment in a tenement building in the middle of the city. There are rats, cockroaches, and other critters who live there with you and you share the bathroom down the hall with forty-two other people. To top it off, you pay $2,500 a week in rent! Every Friday at 3:00 pm you hear a pounding on the door and it is your cigar-chewing landlord. He is not a nice man and he has stinky breath, which is especially noticeable when he yells in your face, "Pay what you owe!" When you don't have the money he beats you up.

One day, you hear that the building has been bought by a new landlord, a wonderful and generous man who moves you into the Hilton for six weeks (on his tab) while he refurbishes all the apartments. You return to a brand-new three-bedroom, two-and-a-half bath, fully furnished apartment, complete with satellite-dish hookup. All of this for $25 per month! Can you feel the difference in your life? One Friday afternoon you are sitting in front of the fireplace reading and you hear a familiar pounding on the door. It can't be! Your stomach tightens and when you answer the door— your old landlord. "Pay what you owe!" he spits out. What do you do? Do you have any legal obligation to pay him rent? Are you still controlled by your fear of him? What would you say to that old landlord? (Note how this follows what Paul tells us to do in verses 12–13):

- "I refuse to let you tyrannize me any longer!"
- "I have nothing more to do with you and I will not pay you one red cent!"
- "I am under new management and he alone deserves what I have!"

So, who are you anyway? If you are in Christ, your baptism symbolizes that you have a new identity not based upon your past but based upon his past. You are not an addict, a pornographer, an abuser, a victim, an adulterer, etc. That is who you were in your Adam-nature, but, in Christ, you are righteous, beloved, and alive to God. The guilt of your past was crucified with Christ and your new identity was begun at his resurrection. The truth of this may not hit your feelings but it must govern your mind. You no longer owe anything to your former life and should not be deceived into thinking that you have any other obligation than to live a new life totally dedicated to serving the Lord Jesus who saved you.

B. THE REIGN OF SIN BROKEN BY OUR BECOMING SLAVES OF GOD (6:15–23)

Review

What happens when you look through the wrong end of a telescope? It defeats the very purpose of the instrument because it makes the object of your study look even further away. This is what many Christians do when they study the work of Christ. They earnestly believe that Jesus died for their forgiveness and that someday they will be sinless like him. However, they do not see that the work of Christ has been brought near to us now and affects our present struggle with sin.

We have properly looked through the telescope of Romans and have seen through the poverty of our own biographies that the unfathomable riches of Christ have been brought near in the gospel. In ourselves, we share the guilt of Adam and are sinners by nature and practice. In Christ, we share his righteousness and are forgiven by mercy and grace. In ourselves, we are dominated by sin and under condemnation of God's law. In Christ, sin is no longer the dominating principle of our lives "for we are no longer under law but under grace" (6:14).

Preview

Remember that 6:1–14 began: "What shall we say, then? Shall we go on sinning so that grace may increase?" (NIV) Paul answers that question with a resounding "By no means!" He then goes on to speak about such an incompatibility because of our faith-union with Christ evidenced through our baptism. He begins this new section in 6:15 in essentially the same way: "What then? Shall we sin because we are not under law but under grace? By no means!" (NIV). Instead of using the analogy of baptism, Paul proceeds to demonstrate the incompatibility of living in sin while being a Christian by the analogy of slavery.

> What Paul does in this second half of Romans 6 is to draw out the
> logic of our conversion, as in the first half he has drawn out the logic
> of our baptism. . . . Since through baptism we were united to Christ,
> and in consequence are dead to sin and alive to God, how can we
> possibly live in sin? Since through our conversion we offered our-
> selves to God to be his slaves, and as the consequence are committed
> to obedience, how can we possibly claim freedom to sin?[3]

Thus, being a Christian has moral implications! Right-standing
with God yields right living; justification yields sanctification; faith yields
obedience.

Verse 16

"Don't you know that when you offer yourselves to someone to obey him
as slaves, you are slaves to the one you obey—whether you are slaves to
sin, which leads to death, or slaves to obedience, which leads to righteousness?" (NIV). The Romans were familiar with a particular type of slavery
that was voluntary in nature. It was very much like the indentured servants
of the American Colonial period, where poor folks or immigrants would
voluntarily place themselves in the service of another in order to be housed
and fed, and to garner wages to be used in establishing a new life for themselves. Such people who voluntarily entered this form of slavery were under
no delusions that they could at the same time maintain their freedom or
"moonlight" for another master. So it is when we were converted to Christ,
we voluntarily offered ourselves to God as his slaves and with that came the
obligation of obedience. We do not owe obedience to anyone else because
we can only be slaves of one person at a time.

Jesus said a similar thing in Matthew 6:24: "No one can have two masters. Either he will hate the one and love the other or he will be devoted
to the one and despise the other" (NIV). Since it is impossible for me to
have more than one master, it will be obvious who (what) my master is by
watching my actions.

In John 8, Jesus said that if a person came to know the truth about
him it would set that person free. The Jewish religious leaders responded
(vv. 33–34): "We are Abraham's descendants and have never been slaves of
anyone. How can you say that we will be set free?" Jesus replied, "I tell you
the truth, everyone who sins [present tense] is a slave to sin" (NIV). The

---

3. Stott, *Romans*, 182–83.

Pharisees vehemently protested that they were free while, at the same time, their behavior (of rejecting Christ) clearly demonstrated the opposite—that they were slaves to sin.

I can say I am a Christian and that I have offered myself to Jesus Christ, but it is whether I obey him or not that will validate or invalidate the truth of my profession. God's grace is free, but does not set me free to live as I please. It sets me free in order to live in obedience to him. I am free, but I am not freed to do anything I want. I am free from the condemnation of the law and the slavery to my sinful (Adam) nature, but I have not been freed to live unto myself.

Verses 17–18

"But thanks be to God that though you used to be slaves to sin, you whole-heartedly obeyed the form of teaching to which you were entrusted. You have been set free from sin and have become slaves of righteousness" (NIV). Paul reminds his readers of the significant change that has already taken place in their lives. Look at the verbs:

"You used to be slaves of sin"—in the *imperfect* tense, which implies what we once were by nature. According to Paul there are only two slaveries, to sin and to God. Our conversion has moved us from one slavery to another.

"You whole-heartedly obeyed"—in the *aorist* tense, which emphasizes a point at which a radical decision was made. Notice also that these believers were entrusted to the form of teaching (apostolic instruction) and not vice versa. "One expects the doctrine to be handed over to the hearers and not the hearers to the doctrine. But Christians are not masters of a tradition; they are themselves created by the word of God and remain in subjection to it."[4]

"You have been set free from sin"—in the *aorist passive* tense, which again emphasizes a decisive point in their lives. However, it was not their action that is in view, but rather what God did for them. He rescued them from sin, and he bought them out of the slave market of sin into his own service, which is described in this last phrase: "You have become slaves to righteousness." Once again, there are only two slaveries, each having its own consequence:

4. Barrett, *Epistle to the Romans*, 132

Slaves of Sin	Slaves of God
6:19 "offer" (aorist tense)—dedicate your body parts to impurity and enter a process of ever-increasing wickedness	6:19 "offer" (aorist tense)—dedicate your body parts to righteous living and grow in ever-increasing holiness (6:13; 12:1)
6:20–21 freedom from the control of righteousness, resulting in the benefits of shame and death	6:22 freedom from the control of sin, resulting in the benefits of holiness and eternal life
6:23 death is the *wage* (*opsonia*—rations paid to soldiers, pocket money given to slaves); in Adam, you always receive what your sin deserves	6:23 eternal life is the *gift*—in Christ, you always receive what you don't deserve

Here then are two slaveries, two lives, two freedoms compared. To illustrate these two freedoms, take a funnel and turn it so that the large end is up. It looks like a lot of freedom but as you progress into the funnel your options gradually narrow until you reach the constricted end. This is like the "freedom" that the world has to offer; it looks liberating but ends up in slavery.

Now turn the funnel upside down. As you look at the narrow end it looks pretty restrictive, doesn't it? But as you progress into it, things really begin to open up. This is the "freedom" that God has to offer. We begin by offering ourselves to God as his slave and end up by experiencing liberation from the dominating influence of the flesh. Remember, freedom is not the right to do as I please, but the power (ability) to do as I ought.

John Stott has a very practical exercise that can help us apply the lessons of what we have studied in Romans 6:

> So, in practice we should be constantly reminding ourselves who we are. We need to learn to talk to ourselves and ask ourselves questions: "Don't you know the meaning of your conversion and baptism? Don't you know that you have been united to Christ in his death and resurrection? Don't you know that you have been enslaved to God and have committed yourself to his obedience? Don't you know these things? Don't you know who you are?" We must go on pressing ourselves with such questions, until we reply to ourselves: "Yes, I know who I am, a new person in Christ, and by the grace of God I shall live accordingly."[5]

---

5. Stott, *Romans*, 187.

C. THE BELIEVER'S RELATIONSHIP
TO THE MORAL LAW (7:1–6)

Review

In Christ, I have not only received a new identity, having been declared righteous in the sight of God, but I am also freed from the miserable bondage of *the evil one* who uses the law against me to keep me under condemnation. I no longer need to beat myself up because of my sin but now I am free to properly deal with the remnant of my old nature (the flesh, the Adam nature), which no longer has any authority over me.

Preview

Paul, in 6:14, said: "for sin shall have dominion over you, for you are not under Law but under grace." He also said, in 1 Corinthians 15:56, "The sting of death is sin, and the strength of sin is the Law." These two verses help us to understand that the power of sin's mastery over us consists of keeping us under the illusion of the condemning power of the law. To put it another way, we live under bondage because we continue to be deceived into thinking that acceptance with God is gained by our own efforts. However, whenever we try to curry God's favor through our performance, we find that it creates greater guilt and condemnation because it never seems good enough. Paul describes the tyranny of this illusion in Romans 7:1–6:

Verse 1: Principle

"The Law has dominion over a man as long as he lives."

Verses 2–3: Illustration

> For the woman who has a husband is bound by the law to her husband as long as he lives; but if the husband dies, she is released from the law of the husband. So then if, while her husband lives she marries another man, she will be called an adulteress; but if her husband dies, she is free from that law, so that she is no adulteress, though she has married another man. Thus, a woman is

contractually bound by law to her husband. However, if the husband dies, the woman is free from the contract and can marry another.[6]

Notice that as Paul begins to apply this principle to the believer, he changes the analogy but the principle remains the same: "the Law has dominion over a man as long as he lives."

Verses 4–5: Application

> Therefore, my brethren, you also have become dead to the law through the Body of Christ, that you might be married to another—to Him who was raised from the dead, that we might bear fruit to God. For when we were in the flesh, the sinful passions, which were aroused by the law, were at work in our members to bear fruit for death.

According to Paul, the only way we could be free from the accusation and condemnation of the law, which is pictured by marriage, is by death. How did we die to the law? We died when Christ died on the cross for us. Remember, Christ's personal history becomes my personal history, through faith. This is what our baptism signifies according to Romans 6:1–14.

Let me explain how our death frees us from the condemnation of law by the following illustration. Imagine that you were convicted of a capital offense and sentenced by the law to be executed. The chemical was injected into your veins and you were history. In the morgue, however, you rose from the dead, found some clothes and decided to head home. You were seen walking downtown and someone called the cops. They arrested you and brought you before the judge. He would have to release you. Why? You already paid the penalty for your crime and you cannot be convicted or punished for that same crime again—a form of double jeopardy. Your death released you from the law.

In Christ, you died to the guilt and penalty of the law of God. "For through the law I died to the law so that I might live for God. I have been crucified with Christ; it is no longer I who live, but Christ lives in me; and the *life* which I now live in the flesh I live by faith in the Son of God, who

6. This text should not be used as a proof-text against divorce for any reason because of Paul's claim that only death can end a marriage. Such a view would bring him into conflict with "the exception clause" of Jesus in Matthew 19:9 and the implications of his own teaching in 1 Corinthians 7:10–16.

loved me and gave Himself for me" (Gal 2:19, 20). In Christ (your new husband), you now have a new principle of life working within, the very life of Jesus Christ. You once lived under the bondage of death and all of your deeds reflected that bondage. Now you live out your new married life in the freedom of Christ's resurrected life, and all your deeds should reflect his character and bear fruit for God. This is why Paul wraps up his thought by saying:

Verse 6: Conclusion

> But now we have been delivered from the law, having died to what we were held by, so that we serve in newness of the Spirit and not in oldness of the letter.

Release from the law does not mean we can go out and live as we please. But it does mean that we are no longer under the condemning power of a performance-based relationship to God but now in a grace-based relationship to him. No longer married to Mr. Law but to Mr. Grace. Now we serve our God out of a heart of sincere love, not out of duty and by the book. Not like the man who felt it was very important to tithe and said, "I tithe 10% of my income and not a penny more!"

Does this mean that the Christian no longer has anything to do with the moral law of God? As Paul would say, "by no means!" It merely means that the law has a different function in the believer's life. Listen to Samuel Bolton (1606–54): "For believers, the Law has been abrogated in respect to its power to justify or condemn, but it remains in full force to direct us in our lives. It condemns sin in the faithful though it cannot condemn the faithful for sin."[7]

Thus, the law of God remains the same; what has changed is the reason for obeying it: not to earn God's love but to show our love to God. Jesus said, "If you love me, keep my commandments. . . . He who has my commandments and keeps them, it is he who loves me. . . . If anyone loves me, he will keep my word" (John 14:15, 21, 23).

It is the Christian who has the ability, because of the indwelling Holy Spirit, to keep the moral law of God according to its true spiritual (7:14) intention. John Calvin has an insightful observation on the moral law:

7. Bolton, *Bounds of Christian Freedom*, 25.

> It must be observed . . . that the commands and prohibitions always imply more than the words express in this precept, "Thou shalt not kill," the common sense of mankind will perceive nothing more than we ought to abstain from all acts of injury to others, and from all desire to commit any such acts. I maintain that it also implies, that we should do every thing that we possibly can towards the preservation of the life of our neighbor.[8]

In other words, flip all the negatives of the Ten Commandments over into positives (e.g., "Thou shalt not steal" into "Thou shalt give to your neighbor") and you will grasp the type of righteousness that pleases God. And it is the Christian who has the ability to render this kind of obedience because of the new birth (Jer 31:33; Ezek 36:26, 27; 1 Pet 1:3–4; 2 Pet 1:3–4)—not yet perfectly but characteristically. If the moral law functions as a guide to the believer for loving obedience, what is the purpose of the law for the unbeliever? We will deal with this question in the next section.

D. THE PURPOSE OF THE MORAL LAW IN THE LIFE OF THE UNBELIEVER (7:7–13)

Review

Paul establishes the principle that the believer has died to the claims of the law, through faith-union with Christ. This does not mean we become lawless. It does mean that because of our "marriage" to Christ we have the ability to obey the law, not as an external performance, but from a heart changed by his grace.

Preview

Paul moves to a new thought in 7:7–13. He clarifies what the unbeliever's relationship is to the moral law of God. He does this by using his own experience before he became a Christian. We know this because he switches over to the use of the past tense. One of the key things he points out is the unbeliever's tendency to blame the moral law without seeing his own sinful condition. So he proceeds to set forth several purposes of the law:

---

8. Calvin, *Institutes*, 323.

Verse 7

> "What shall we say then? Is the law sin? Certainly not! On the contrary, I would not have come to know sin except through the law; for I would not have known coveteousness unless the law had said, 'You shall not covet.'"

The law is not evil—it is not the problem. In fact, the law is good because without it Paul would not have been able to identify that he was a sinner. So, the first purpose of the law in the life of the unbeliever is that it reveals sin in the sinner. "I would not have come to know sin except through the law." It was not the tenth commandment that caused Paul to covet, rather it was the law that uncovered the covetousness that already existed in his heart. "For by the law comes the knowledge of sin" (3:20).

Verse 8

> But sin, taking an opportunity [*aphorme,* "a base of operations for a military action"] by the commandment, produced in me all manner of evil desire. For apart from the law sin was dead.

The second purpose of the law is to provoke sin. The commandment told Paul not to covet but it produced a rebellious reaction with his sinful nature that made him want to covet all the more. Like a "Quiet Please" sign makes me want to yell; a "Wet Paint" sign makes me want to touch; and someone telling me not to step in the mud puddle makes me want to stomp in it all day. The law is not the problem. It brings out in me the sin that I did not know (or did not want to admit) was there. Without the law, I could actually fool myself into thinking I am not such a bad guy after all. With the law, however, I am made to see my desperate need of forgiveness.

Verse 9

> I was once alive without the law; but when the commandment came, sin revived and I died.

There was a time when Paul actually thought he was just fine apart from the law. "He is speaking of the unperturbed, self-complacent, self-righteous life

73

which he once lived before the turbulent emotions and convictions of sin, described in the two preceding verses, overtook him."[9]

Then the commandment about covetousness came and not only did it stir him up, but put to death his self-complacency—he saw himself under the condemnation of the law. This, then, is the third purpose of the law: to condemn sin.

Verse 10–11

> And the commandment, which was to bring life, I found to bring death. For sin, taking occasion by the commandment deceived me, and by it killed me.

Paul underscores the deceptive nature of sin; it turned the law, which was originally given to show the way of life and righteousness, into something that produced condemnation and death. In other words, his sinful nature led him to think that all he needed was to do right (performance) and he would be right (acceptance). But it was all a big lie, and through this deception he was killed ("I died," v. 9)—he experienced the condemnation of the law. The murderer wasn't the law, but his sinful nature.

Verse 12

> Therefore the law is holy, and the commandment is holy and just and good.

Paul's conclusion here is that in spite of the fact that the law reveals, provokes, and condemns sin, it is still good. The law was not responsible for his sin. His sinful human nature was responsible. And this sinful nature used his performance-based mentality toward the law as a weapon for destroying Paul after promising it to be a vehicle for saving him.

Verse 13

> Has then what is good become death to me? Certainly not! But sin, that it might appear sin, was producing death in me through what

9. Murray, *Romans*, 251.

is good, so that sin through the commandment might become exceedingly sinful.

If you break a law and are punished, you cannot blame the law. It would be your fault; your sin earned you that sentence. The sooner you realize that, the better you will be able to deal with the real issues in your life that caused you to break the law in the first place. So Paul says that he could never blame the law of God for his condemnation because that law was just doing its proper work of showing him how utterly sinful his sinful nature was.

Most convicts don't deserve to be in jail, or so they say. Most people who get caught speeding "were not really going that fast." That standardized test that I failed was "a bad test." And so when God's law commands us not to lie, cheat, steal, shack up or snuff out, we may rebel against it and find it old-fashioned, confining, and inadequate in dealing with the complex moral dilemmas of our post-modern age. But that very reaction to the absolute moral commands of God means that the law is doing its proper work. It is revealing the sin that lurks in my heart, parading itself as self-righteous and spiritual and telling me, "You're fine, don't listen to those negative messages; you're better than most," while leading me down the path of self-destruction. I must wake up and listen to the law, for it is condemning that slimy, sneaky, deceptive nature of mine (inherited from Adam) and offering me a better way, the way of grace and forgiveness that comes through faith in what Jesus Christ has done for me by his death and resurrection.

In summary, 7:1–6 shows us that our death to the law (in Christ) has released us from the bondage of a performance-based relationship to God. Now we are free to serve him, not because we have to in order to earn his acceptance, but because we choose to according to the work of the Spirit in our hearts. Does this mean that the law of God is evil because it condemns us? In 7:7–13, Paul looks back on his life before Christ and now sees that the law was performing its good and powerful work of revealing the real culprit: his sinful human nature. Without this exposure of his true nature, Paul would have continued to believe the deception that he was quite all right on his own and did not need a savior.

E. THE BELIEVER'S STRUGGLE WITH THE
REMNANT OF THE OLD ADAM-NATURE (7:14–25)

Review

Our death (in Christ) to the law has released us from the performance-based mentality of trying to earn acceptance with God. Instead, we are now in a grace-based relationship where we are free to serve God, not by a legalistic obedience but by one that proceeds from a willing heart. This does not mean that the law is evil or irrelevant to those who are in Christ. On the contrary, the law is good and it does its good work by showing the unbeliever his sin and need of a savior.

Preview

Paul uses the past tense in verses 7–13 to describe his pre-Christian relationship to the law. In verses 14–25, he switches to the present tense indicating that his struggle with the flesh is something that he is now undergoing as a person who is in Christ. Some commentators, such as Schreiner, believe that Paul is still describing the experience of the non-believer. However, the twenty-six first-person verbs in this section, as well as a redeemed perspective on the law, are powerful hints that Paul is referring to his present experience as a believer. In this section, therefore, Paul vividly portrays his struggle of sanctification against his own version of the flesh. (Compare Philippians 3:1–7.)

For many, Paul's experience finds its mark in their own. How many of us have had significant victory over temptation and old patterns of behavior when we first came to Christ, but then these old beasts reared their ugly heads and almost out of nowhere had us slipping and sliding back into behavior we thought we had long since conquered? It is this scenario that Paul is addressing, once again by using his own personal experience.

There are two very simple observations that will greatly clarify what some have found confusing about Paul's thought. First, Paul repeats himself in order to emphasize his point: he describes his struggle in 7:14–17 and then repeats himself in 7:18–20.

Verse 14:   "We know that the law is spiritual; but I am unspiritual (sarki-nos), sold as a slave to sin."

Verse 15:   "I do not understand what I do; for what I want to do I do not do, but what I hate to do."

Verses 16–17:"And if I do what I do not want to do, I agree that the law is good. As it is, it is no longer I myself who do it, but it is the sin living in me."

And then Paul repeats the struggle:

Verse 18:   "I know that nothing good lives in me, that is, in my sinful nature [*sarki*]."

Verse 19:   "For what I do is not the good I want to do; no, the evil I do not want to do— this I keep on doing."

Verse 20:   "Now if I do what I don't want to do, it is no longer I who do it, but it is sin living in me that does it (NIV)."

The second observation is that Paul uses a lot of "I's"—twenty of them in seven verses. It is helpful to notice the presence of what commentators have called a "divided or split I." In other words, Paul acknowledges the presence of two opposite identities struggling within him. James Dunn attributes the "split I" to the fact that the believer is "stretched between the old epoch of sin and the new epoch of grace."[10] The Christian is caught between the double reality of the "already" (having the new Christ nature within) and the "not yet" (being perfected in righteousness, but still contending with some of the old software left in the new computer). John Stott clarifies things further by the suggestion that Paul in this section is in the process of making a discovery.[11] Notice the progression of Paul's thought:

- vv. 14, 18: Paul's initial assessment of his struggle is that he is just a sinner who doesn't have the ability in himself to overcome the slavery to his sinful nature ("nothing good lives in me").

- vv. 15, 19: His struggle produces confusion because he doesn't understand why he can't do the things he should, even though he desires to do them. This is what John Stott calls the existence of the "divided I." "For there is an 'I' which wants the good and hates the evil, and there is an 'I' which acts perversely, doing what is hated and not doing what

10. Dunn, *Romans*, 408.
11. Stott, *Romans*, 211–15.

is wanted. The conflict is between desire and performance; the will is there, but the ability is not."[12]

- vv. 16, 17, 20: His confusion produces a discovery. He begins to realize something he hadn't known before, that he is not the real culprit. Rather it is something that is alien to his new identity and dwells within him. "The real I, 'I myself', is the 'I' which loves and wants the good and hates the evil, for that is its essential orientation. Therefore, the 'I' which does the opposite (doing what I hate and not doing what I want) is not the real or genuine 'I,' but rather a usurper, namely, indwelling sin, or *sarx* (the flesh)."[13]

In other words, Paul says, "Wait a minute, it isn't 'I' who creates this conflict because 'I' want to love and serve God (v. 22). The problem is the remnant of my old Adam nature, the flesh, which wages war against who 'I' really am in Christ!" You see, even though a person is a new creature in Christ, he occupies the same body, has the same brain with its patterns and memory, lives with the same family history as he had before he became a Christian. While these things no longer define the believer or have authority over him, the Accuser (Revelation 12:10) will often try to use these old patterns to neutralize the believer's witness and undermine his assurance before God.

Here is an interesting analogy in Neil Anderson's book, which helps clarify the duality.[14] If you were walking along the street and a little dog came along and grabbed onto your leg, would you take a stick and beat yourself or the dog? Can you imagine seeing anything more ridiculous than a guy beating himself with a stick while that little mutt was still chomping on his leg? Yet, if Paul had not made this discovery about the indwelling remnant of the old nature, he would have continued to beat himself up, and the only cry that would have come from his lips would have been: "O wretched man that I am! Who will rescue me from this body of death?" (v. 24, NIV).

The word wretched (*talaipooros*) is a military term, which means exhausted and miserable from the battle. Paul shares his misery and exhaustion from beating himself up in his struggle with sin. How? Perhaps he did this by trying to do better, by memorizing more Scripture, by vows, fasting, and disciplines. However, remember the context—the law cannot save, it

12. Stott, *Romans*, 212.
13. Stott, *Romans*, 212.
14. Anderson, *Bondage Breaker*, 51.

cannot give power to overcome the flesh. John Owen said that "duties are an excellent food for an unhealthy soul, but they are no medicine for a sick soul."[15] I believe Paul is exhausted from trying to deal with his old patterns of behavior in his own power by stepping up his performance level. Again, John Owen: "A soul under the conviction from the law is pressed to fight against sin, but has no strength for the combat."[16]

This is so important! We cannot overcome the flesh by any performance-based activity, like involving ourselves in church activities, or giving more money to help the missionary enterprise, or ramping up our spiritual disciplines. These are good things (like the law is good), but when used as a strategy to overcome the flesh, they will only serve to condemn and exhaust. They will only serve to beat up on ourselves instead of the dog.

However, since Paul realizes that it is the "dog" of his sinful nature and not his true self that inflicts such pain and confusion, he can turn his attention to the real culprit and not beat himself up any longer. This is why his second cry is so important:

Verse 25

"Thanks be to God—through Jesus Christ our Lord!" (NIV). At first glance this cry may seem anticlimactic—it's not even a full sentence. Then we realize that Paul is reiterating what he already said in chapter 6; our deliverance from the struggle with our sinful flesh comes as we affirm who we are in Jesus Christ, and that our sinful self and the temptations of the flesh no longer define or control us because we have the indwelling Holy Spirit. It also indicates that our ultimate deliverance from this struggle will be at our resurrection. In the meantime, remember how we treat the old landlord lest we slip back under the illusion that he has authority over us: "No, you are no longer my master. I owe you nothing; I am under new management. I will obey only him." Such a response works because by it we cooperate with the Holy Spirit who releases within us the very life of Christ. This new life is the subject of Romans 8.

The justified believer, while still in a struggle with sin, recognizes that this struggle does not define her identity. We are new creatures in Christ who still contend with our leftover sinful nature. The victory is to be found

---

15. Owen, *Temptation and Sin*, 18.
16. Owen, *Temptation and Sin*, 20.

in the position of grace that we occupy in Christ and the power of the indwelling Holy Spirit, who enables us to do the good that we wish (v. 19).

> And I will give you a new heart, and a new spirit I will put within you. And I will remove the heart of stone . . . and give you a heart of flesh. And I will put my Spirit within you, and cause you to walk in my statutes and be careful to obey my rules.
>
> —Ezekiel 36:26–27, ESV

VI

The Victory of the Believer by the Holy Spirit and Security in Christ 8:1–39

A. THE MINISTRY OF THE HOLY SPIRIT (8:1–27)

Review

THOUGH THE JUSTIFIED BELIEVER still struggles with the remnants of the Adam nature, victory in this struggle is found in the position of grace he/ she occupies in Christ. This is why the overarching theme of Romans 8 is the security of the believer. Notice that the chapter begins with no condemnation to those who are in Christ Jesus and ends with no separation from God's love in Christ Jesus.

Preview

The following is an old children's rhyme attributed to various authors (John Bunyan, John Berridge, Ralph Erskine) that sums up the essence of Romans 8:

To run and walk the law demands
But gives me neither feet nor hands.
Better news the Gospel brings
It bids me fly and gives me wings!

There is therefore now no condemnation to those who are in
Christ Jesus, who do not walk according to the flesh, but according to the Spirit. For the law of the Spirit of life in Christ Jesus
has made me free from the law of sin and death. For what the law
could not do in that it was weak through the flesh, God did by
sending His own Son in the likeness of sinful flesh, on account of
sin: He condemned sin in the flesh, that the righteous requirement
of the law might be fulfilled in us who do not walk according to the
flesh but according to the Spirit. (vv. 1–4)

A great secondary title for this section would be "The Law of Pneuma-
Dynamics." *Pneuma* is the Greek word for "spirit." Just as a huge C-5 air-
plane can seemingly defy the law of gravity and fly because of the law of
aerodynamics, so the person in Christ can overcome the gravitational pull
of sin and live righteously by the power of the indwelling Holy Spirit. Let
me reiterate that those of us who are in Christ have the identity of being
justified (declared holy, righteous, and blameless) in God's sight because
of what Christ has done for us. Flowing out of this positional righteousness is the work of the Holy Spirit in us called *sanctification*, giving us the
very ability to live righteously. In other words, we were *justified* so that we
might be *sanctified*. The purpose of God's action in Christ was to produce
an obedient people. As John Stott says, "This is not perfectionism; it is simply to say that obedience is a necessary and possible aspect of Christian
discipleship."[1]

This obedience is accomplished through the indwelling Holy Spirit.
Up to this point, Paul has mentioned the Holy Spirit only five times. However, in chapter 8 alone, he mentions the Spirit twenty times, more than
any other chapter in the Bible. This is where we can learn much about the
Holy Spirit.

1. The Holy Spirit guarantees our holiness.

For those who live according to the flesh set their minds on the
things of the flesh, but those who live according to the Spirit, the
things of the Spirit. For to be carnally minded is death, but to be

1. Stott, *Romans*, 221.

> spiritually minded is life and peace. Because the carnal mind is
> enmity against God; for it is not subject to the law of God, nor
> indeed can be. So then, those who are in the flesh cannot please
> God. But you are not in the flesh but in the Spirit, if indeed the
> Spirit of God dwells in you. Now if anyone does not have the Spirit
> of Christ, he is not His. (vv. 5–9)

Notice how Paul sets up a contrast between believers and unbelievers:

Unbelievers: those who "live according to the flesh" (v. 4), who "set
their minds on the things of the flesh" (v. 5), and who are dead spiritually
and therefore hostile to God and his law (vv. 7–8). The flesh denotes our
sinful nature. Although the flesh still influences the Christian, it should no
longer dominate him nor characterize him like it did before he was made
alive in Christ. Unbelievers, however, are controlled by this sinful nature
(their being in Adam), and do not have the ability to submit to God and to
live in a way pleasing to him. They are dead, blind, and deaf to the things
of God. They can have "spirituality" and can do good things, but only as a
parody of the real thing because they do not have the true "Spirit."

Believers: those who are believers live "according to the Spirit" (vv. 4,
5, 6, 9). The person in Christ does not characteristically live by the values or
dictates of the flesh (although he still struggles with the flesh), but the Holy
Spirit regulates his life. The word for mind, *phroneo*, means "driving force"
or "ambition." The believer is one who has been changed to such an extent
that the things with which he is now ultimately concerned are the things of
God. Thus, the presence of the Holy Spirit in one's life defines who is truly
in Christ. The Spirit is also the source of our dignity, holiness, and happiness. Without him, we would still be dead, dominated, and desensitized to
God.

2. The Spirit guarantees our resurrection. Notice that these two verses
begin with "if." Paul is not speaking hypothetically nor is he expressing
doubt. Rather, he is stating two major results of the indwelling Holy Spirit
in the believer's life.

> And if Christ is in you, the body is dead because of sin, but the
> Spirit is life because of righteousness. But if the Spirit of Him who
> raised Jesus from the dead dwells in you, He who raised Christ
> from the dead will also give life to your mortal bodies through His
> Spirit who dwells in you. (vv. 10–11)

Verse 10: "And if Christ is in you, your body is dead because of sin,
yet your spirit is alive because of righteousness." (Notice the interchange

of terms between Christ and the Holy Spirit. Christ dwells in us through the Spirit.) Paul is saying that even though our bodies are in the process of dying and are, in fact, destined to death because of sin, the Holy Spirit is very much alive and is in the process of renewing us. "Therefore, we do not lose heart. Even though our outward man is perishing, yet the inward man is being renewed day by day" (2 Cor 4:16).

Verse 11: "But if the Spirit of Him who raised Jesus from the dead is living in you, He who raised Christ from the dead will also give life to your mortal bodies." Death is not our ultimate destiny. Someday, the Spirit will actually effect the resurrection of our bodies. Paul teaches in 1 Corinthians 15:35–49 that this will include a complete transformation of our bodies to the extent that they will no longer be mortal, subject to decay, disease and death. Christianity knows nothing of a glorified state filled with disembodied spirits. Our ultimate hope lies not in escaping our bodies but in the transformation of them into a new and glorious vehicle for our transformed personality.[2]

3. The Holy Spirit demands an obligation.

> Therefore, brethren, we are debtors—not to the flesh, to live according to the flesh. For if you live according to the flesh you will die; but if by the Spirit you put to death the deeds of the body, you will live. (vv. 12–13)

"Therefore, brothers, we are debtors." When it comes to our justification, it is completely a work of Christ on our behalf. We have nothing to do with it. How could we when we were dead in our sins? However, when it comes to our sanctification, we must cooperate with the Holy Spirit in the process. Through our new nature, we have the ability as well as the responsibility (obligation) to make choices that please God. Such a choice unleashes the sanctifying work of the Holy Spirit, which empowers us to live in such a way that pleases God. Look at the active language that is used to describe our part in this process:

- We must mind (pay attention to) the things of the Spirit (v. 5).

- We must walk according to the Spirit and not the flesh (v. 4).

- We must through the Spirit put to death the deeds of the flesh (v. 13).

This is what the Puritans called the *mortification of the flesh*. The concept is based upon the verb (*thanatoo*), which means "death." Literally, it

2. Stott, *Romans*, 227.

means handing someone over to be executed. In this context it means to decisively repudiate the passions and desires of our leftover flesh, or every day to "preside at our own funeral" as my friend Rev. Richard Burr used to say. John Owen describes mortification this way:

> To kill a man, or any living thing, is to take away the principle of all his strength, vigour, and power, so that he cannot exert, or put forth any proper actions of his own; so it is in this case. Indwelling sin is compared to a person, a living person, called "the old man," with his faculties, and properties, his wisdom, craft, subtlety, strength; this, says the apostle, must be killed, put to death, mortified—that is, have its power, life, vigour, and strength to produce its effects, taken away by the Spirit. . . . And the "old man" is thence said to be "crucified with Christ," and ourselves to be "dead" with him . . . initially in regeneration . . . but the whole work is by degrees to be carried on towards [completion] all our days.[3]

4. The Holy Spirit witnesses to our adoption.

> For as many as are led by the Spirit of God, these are sons of God. For you did not receive the spirit of bondage again to fear, but you received the Spirit of adoption by whom we cry out, "Abba, Father." The Spirit Himself bears witness with our spirit that we are children of God, and if children, then heirs—heirs of God and joint heirs with Christ, if indeed we suffer with Him, that we may also be glorified together. (vv. 14–17)

"For as many who are led of the Spirit of God are sons of God." The moral character of the Christian's life (those who are led by the Spirit of God) is a demonstration of our very son-ship. God's children exhibit the family trait of holiness. Our obedience is not motivated by the fear of God as a divine judge rendering us terrified slaves in his presence. Instead, our relationship to God has been changed completely and forever by the work of Christ. Now we are granted the status of "sons" and our obedience flows out of the freedom of our son-ship. Literally, v. 15b says, "but you received the Spirit of adoption." This refers to the practice found in Greek and Roman culture of a slave being adopted as a son in a childless household in order to perpetuate the family line. So, we who were once sold in the slave-market of sin have now been adopted into the very family of God by his sovereign grace. Regeneration gives us a new nature. Adoption grants us a new status and the Holy Spirit is our internal witness to this new status.

3. Owen, *Temptation and Sin*, 8.

The objective faith-fact of our adoption as sons is further witnessed to by two internal faith-realities. First, an intimacy of relationship with God: and "by Him [the Holy Spirit] we cry 'Abba, Father'" (v. 15c). This term was never found on the lips of a religious Jew because it was too familiar a term to be applied to God. It was the language of the home, of the little child calling out spontaneously to his daddy. And yet, Jesus used it every time he prayed except for his cry of dereliction from the cross. The Holy Spirit enables us to pray as Jesus did, calling out to our Heavenly Daddy with childlike assurance whether in the midst of worship or in the face of suffering.

Second, it is in the midst of such intimacy of prayer that the Holy Spirit administers a kind of status-consciousness of our relationship to God. In other words, "the Spirit Himself bears witness with our spirit [*symmartyreo*, "witness together with"], that we are children of God" (v. 16). I do not believe that this inward witness of the Holy Spirit is some special experience that we seek in order to attain a certain level of spirituality. The flesh is allergic to simple faith and is always looking for new experiences to validate itself and to gain superiority over others. The context indicates that the witness of the Spirit is common for all Christians in times of suffering (v. 17).

5. The Holy Spirit is the firstfruit of our redemption.

> For I consider that the sufferings of this present time are not worthy to be compared with the glory which shall be revealed in us. For the earnest expectation of the creation eagerly waits for the revealing of the sons of God. For the creation was subjected to futility, not willingly, but because of Him who subjected it in hope; because the creation itself also will be delivered from the bondage of corruption into the glorious liberty of the children of God. For we know that the whole creation groans and labors with birth pangs together until now. Not only that, but we also who have the first-fruits of the Spirit, even we ourselves groan within ourselves, eagerly waiting for the adoption, the redemption of our body. For we were saved in this hope, but hope that is seen is not hope; for why does one still hope for what he sees? But if we hope for what we do not see, we eagerly wait for it with perseverance. (vv. 18–25)

Paul acknowledges the reality of suffering in this world. Notice the repetition of the word "groan." Creation itself *groans* together and travails, like a woman in childbirth, because of the bondage to which it has been subjected because of the fall of man (vv. 20–21). I understand this to mean that all of creation has been affected by the entrance of sin into the world (Gen 3:17–18). The word *stenazo* ("groan") can mean either to cry or to sigh: the cry of pain because creation "is raw in tooth and claw"; the sigh of waiting in hope for its rescue. And when will this be? The creation waits in eager expectation for the sons of God to be revealed (v. 19). In other words, creation itself will share in the glory of God's completed work of salvation in all those who are his children; just like it shared in the curse of Adams sin (Isa 11:6–9; 2 Pet 3:13; Rev 21:1–5).

"And not only the creation, but we ourselves, who have the first fruits of the Spirit, groan inwardly as we wait eagerly for our adoption as sons, the redemption of our bodies" (v. 23, ESV). We groan (cry) because of the suffering we endure due to the effects of sin on our bodies, our families, our world. We also groan (sigh) because we have experienced a taste of eternity through the ministry of the Holy Spirit and we long for the final phase of our salvation (1 Pet 1:3–5). And this salvation is inevitable because we possess the Holy Spirit, the first fruit (*aparche*, "the beginning") of what is yet to come.

At the Feast of Harvest or Firstfruits, Israel brought the beginning of her crops as an offering to the Lord of all that was to come. When did God choose to send the Holy Spirit upon the church? At Pentecost, also known as the Feast of Harvest or Firstfruits. God was telling his church that the coming of the Holy Spirit was just the beginning of the full harvest of the cross that awaits the believer when Christ returns. In 2 Corinthians 1:22, Paul uses the term *arrabon* to describe the Spirit's presence as a deposit or pledge; it could also be translated *engagement ring*. The Holy Spirit is God's engagement ring; his pledge that he will make good on his promises to his bride, the church. What a glorious future awaits the believer! "For our light affliction, which is but for a moment, is working for us an eternal weight of glory" (2 Cor 4:17).

6. The Holy Spirit helps us to pray in our weakness.

> Likewise the Spirit also helps in our weaknesses. For we do not know what we should pray for as we ought, but the Spirit Himself makes intercession for us with groanings which cannot be uttered. Now He who searches the hearts knows what the mind of the Spirit is, because He makes intercession for the saints according to the will of God. (vv. 26–27)

Often in the midst of our suffering and pain we cry out to God. It is not a coherent petition but more like the cry of a little child. We do not even know what it is for which we should ask. It is at the point of this *weakness* that the Holy Spirit becomes our intercessor. He does so with groans too deep for words. Here is the word "groan" again. First, creation groans, then we who have the Spirit groan, and now the Spirit groans. It seems to indicate that at times, when we do not know how to pray, the Holy Spirit prays for us in sighs too deep for words. The Father discerns these unarticulated prayers as he searches our hearts because he knows the intentions of the Spirit and that they are always agreeable to the will of God. Some people, like Calvin, do not believe it is the Spirit that groans but rather that he intercedes through our groaning. Whatever the interpretation, we have here a wonderful encouragement to pray. The Holy Spirit articulates to the Father precisely that for which we should be praying while we are struggling to manage just a cry or a groan.

In summary of chapter 8, what would our Christian lives be like without the Holy Spirit?

- We would not have the wings to fly above the gravitational pull of our sinful nature.

- We would not have the process of renewal taking place in our lives right now.

- We would not have the hope of the resurrection of our bodies from the dead.

- We would not have any power to cooperate with the Holy Spirit in the process of sanctification; all our attempts at spiritual discipline and resisting sin would end in utter failure.

- We would never have the awareness of our status as sons and daughters of God.

- We would be overwhelmed by the hopelessness of our gut-wrenching existence in this world; we would have no understanding that this is not all there is.

- We would be overwhelmed by our helplessness to pray in times of pain and discouragement; we would have no one to help us as we cry and sigh.

Thank God for his Holy Spirit!

B. THE STEADFAST LOVE OF THE LORD (8:28–39)

Review

We already stated that the overarching theme of Romans 8 is the security of the believer. We saw in the previous section that we are secure because the demands of the law have been fulfilled in Christ so that we are no longer condemned by it, and we have been given the Holy Spirit. The very same Spirit who enables us live holy lives, gives us the hope of resurrection, witnesses to our status as "sons," guarantees that God will make good on all his promises, and helps us to pray in the midst of our weakness.

Preview

In this beautiful and most famous section of Romans, we have emblazoned for us the steadfast love of God portrayed in his irresistible plan of salvation for every believer. John Stott suggests that we see this worked out by Paul as he posits five unshakeable convictions, five undeniable affirmations, and five unanswerable questions.[4]

8:28: Five Unshakeable Convictions

> And we know that all things work together for good to those who love God, to those who are the called according to His purpose.

- God works
- For the good
- In all things
- For those that love him
- Who have been called according to his purpose

Although "all things" is the subject of the sentence, the implication is not that all these things "somehow" work themselves together for the best. Paul believes that God is the Sovereign One who is unceasingly at work in *all things* in order to accomplish his purpose on behalf of his people. This is

---

4. Stott, *Romans*, 246.

also how we define the *good*—not that the circumstances of our lives will always be pleasant, but that they will always accomplish the purposes of God. He saved us and called us to a holy life—not because of anything we have done, but because of his own purpose and grace (Eph 1:5–6; 2 Tim 1:9).

Therefore, the *good* is the fulfillment of God's ultimate purpose for us; the reason why he called us and set his love upon us. We can have an unshakeable conviction that everything in our lives will be used by a Sovereign God to complete in us the work which he began when he called us to himself.

8:29, 30: Five Undeniable Affirmations

> For whom He foreknew, He also predestined to be conformed to the image of His Son, that He might be the firstborn among many brethren. Moreover whom He predestined, these He also called; whom He called, these He also justified; and whom He justified, these He also glorified.

"He foreknew"—This means more than knowing something before it happens. In biblical language the word "to know" is a term of intimacy. We could translate "foreknew" as "to love or to set one's love upon." Look at some of the following passages: Gen 18:19; Exod 2:25; Pss 1:6; 144:3; Jer 1:5; Amos 3:2; Hosea 13:5; Matt 7:23; 1 Cor 8:3; Gal 4:9; 2 Tim 2:19; 1 John 3:1. The term "foreknew" is more than just knowing ahead of time. There is a relational component implied.

"He predestined them to be conformed to the image of His Son"—This term (*proorizo*) simply means "to decide on ahead of time." Predestination does not take away from the responsibility we have to repent and believe the gospel or to grow in our Christlikeness once we do believe. It does, however, place our decision squarely within the context of God's prior determination to grant us such repentance and faith, and upon his resources to live more and more like Jesus. God's grace was not bestowed upon us because he saw some virtuous quality or even some foreseen faith in us before we were chosen.

"And you He made alive, who were dead in trespasses and sins, in which you once walked according to the course of this world, according to the prince of the power of the air, the spirit who now works in the sons of disobedience, among whom also we all once conducted ourselves in the lusts of our flesh, fulfilling the desires of the flesh and of the mind, and were by nature children of wrath, just as the others. But God, who is rich in mercy, because of His great love with which He loved us, even when we were dead in trespasses, made us alive together with Christ [by grace you have been saved]" (Eph 2:1–5).[5]

"He also called"—I believe this does not speak of the general call of the gospel when people are invited to receive Christ. I believe this refers to the "effectual" call of the Holy Spirit which not only summons, but actually enables a person to respond to the gospel. "God's call, since it is effectual, carries with it the operative grace whereby the person called is enabled to answer the call and to embrace Jesus Christ as He is freely offered in the gospel."[6]

"He also justified"—Those who hear the divine summons and open their hearts to the gospel are justified by the work of Christ, acquitted of their sins, and are accepted into the family of God.

"He also glorified"—The very hope of ultimately being brought to glory and having a transfigured body like Christ is put in the same tense (*aorist*) as those things which have already taken place in our relationship to God. The very completion of our salvation is so certain it is seen as already accomplished.[7]

These undeniable affirmations are like an unbreakable chain linking us securely to the undefeatable plan of God for those who are his.

8:31–39: Five Unanswerable Questions

> What then shall we say to these things? If God is for us, who can be against us? He who did not spare His own Son, but delivered Him up for us all, how shall He not with Him also freely give us all things? Who shall bring a charge against God's elect? It is God who justifies. Who is he who condemns? It is Christ who died, and furthermore is also risen, who is even at the right hand of God, who also makes intercession for us. Who shall separate us from the love of Christ? Shall tribulation, or distress, or persecution, or famine, or nakedness, or peril, or sword? As it is written:

> "For Your sake we are killed all day long;

5. For more on God's electing grace, read Ephesians 1:4–14.

6. Murray, *Romans*, 317.

7. Similar emphasis in 1 Peter 1:3–5.

We are accounted as sheep for the slaughter."

> Yet in all these things we are more than conquerors through Him who loved us. For I am persuaded that neither death nor life, nor angels nor principalities nor powers, nor things present nor things to come, nor height nor depth, nor any other created thing, shall be able to separate us from the love of God which is in Christ Jesus our Lord.

Having established this unbreakable chain of God's commitment to our salvation, Paul says, "What shall we say to these things?" He then asks a series of five questions in which he seems to be searching for some "weak link" in the chain or some "glitch" in the plan that might undermine our security. The first four questions have to do with our guilt and self-accusation, acknowledging that we are often our own worst enemies when it comes to the security of our salvation. The last question has to do with the circumstances of life. However, all of these questions are designed to be answered in the negative, underscoring the conviction that nothing can hinder the salvation of God's people.

Question 1: "If God is for us, who can be against us?" Since there is no one greater than God—not parents, not spouse, not conscience, not kings, not Satan, therefore, no one is able to prevent God's plan for his people from being accomplished.

Question 2: "He who did not spare His own Son, but gave Him up for us all, how shall He not with Him also freely give us all things." The greatest gift of Christ implies all other "lesser" gifts. If God spared no expense to make us his, he will spare no expense to keep us his.

Question 3: "Who will bring a charge against God's elect? It is God who justifies." The penalty for our sin was paid by Jesus Christ. There is nothing else that is owed; therefore, any charges brought against us are deceptive and no longer relevant. Note the vision of Zechariah (3:1–5) about Joshua the high priest who was accused by Satan of being unworthy to make atonement for the sins of his people because of his own sin. The Lord himself rebuked the accuser and clothed Joshua in a new garment of righteousness, therefore taking away his reproach and foreshadowing the coming work of Christ (the Branch). Put your name in the place of Joshua's name.

Question 4: "Who is he that condemns? It is Christ who died, and further-more is also risen, who is even at the right hand of God, who makes intercession for us." The only one worthy enough to be my judge is Jesus Christ and he just happens to be my Savior. He died for me (my forgiveness), he rose for me (my victory over sin), and he prays for me (my security).

Question 5: "Who shall separate us from the love of Christ?" Paul offers a list of seven possible circumstances, all of which he had experienced:

- Trouble—outward pressure of personal circumstances
- Hardship—anguish, inward distress
- Persecution—being pursued for the sake of Christ
- Famine—suffering hunger or want
- Nakedness—lack of proper clothing
- Danger—peril, running a risk
- Sword—the short sword (dagger) used by the violent (robbers and insurrectionists)

"Yet in all these things we are more than conquerors through Him who loved us." God does not help us to escape the sufferings of this life, but he helps us to face them victoriously. Paul actually uses the superlative "over-conqueror" to describe the believer in the face of human tragedy. Does this describe you?

In his grand summation, Paul searches the cosmos to see if there is anything able to interfere with God's plan for his children. Notice the couplets which indicate completeness:

- "death nor life"—neither the pain of dying nor the pain of living
- "angels nor principalities"—supernatural beings, neither good nor evil
- "things present nor things to come"—neither present fears nor an uncertain future
- "powers"—natural catastrophe, governmental violence, economic disaster
- "height nor depth"—neither heights of worldly fame and prosperity nor the depths of poverty and worldly abasement

- "nor anything else in all of creation" (just in case there is something we forgot)
- "shall be able to separate us from the love of God which is in Christ Jesus our Lord."

The security of the believer in Romans 8 begins with *no condemnation* and ends with *no separation* and in between is the Holy Spirit. Do you have such assurance of your relationship to God? Upon what are you basing your salvation? Notice that this unending love is found only in Jesus Christ. Is he your Savior?

VII

God's Relationship with Ethnic Israel (9–11)

A. THE REJECTION OF ETHNIC ISRAEL AND GOD'S SOVEREIGNTY (9:1-29)

Review

AFTER CLEARLY STATING THE work of the Holy Spirit and the security of the believer in chapter 8, Paul shares his heart for his people Israel, who have rejected the gospel. He sounds very much like Moses in Exodus 32:30–32 in the face of the Israel's unbelief. This rejection of ethnic Israel is magnified by the incredible eightfold blessing that Israel has experienced. We should not consider this section as new and unrelated to what has come before. Instead, Paul raises the question about how such rejection and unbelief can be explained if God's covenant promises to his chosen never fail as chapter 8 details.

Preview

Paul proceeds in verses 1–5 to explain this unbelief and rejection of ethnic Israel on the basis of God's sovereign decision, not on the failure of God to keep his covenant promise to Abraham.

> I tell the truth in Christ, I am not lying, my conscience also bearing me witness in the Holy Spirit, that I have great sorrow and continual grief in my heart. For I could wish that I myself were accursed from Christ for my brethren, my countrymen according to the flesh, who are Israelites, to whom pertain the adoption, the glory, the covenants, the giving of the law, the service of God, and the promises; of whom are the fathers and from whom, according to the flesh, Christ came, who is over all, the eternally blessed God. Amen.

The key to this section is the last half of verse 6: "For they are not all Israel who are of Israel." This reason is clarified in a series of four statements explaining the unbelief and rejection of Israel.

1. It is not because God is unfaithful (vv. 6–13).

> But it is not that the word of God has taken no effect. For they are not all Israel who are of Israel, nor are they all children because they are the seed of Abraham; but, "In Isaac your seed shall be called." That is, those who are the children of the flesh, these are not the children of God; but the children of the promise are counted as the seed. For this is the word of promise: "At this time I will come and Sarah shall have a son." And not only this, but when Rebecca also had conceived by one man, even by our father Isaac (for the children not yet being born, nor having done any good or evil, that the purpose of God according to election might stand, not of works but of Him who calls), it was said to her, "The older shall serve the younger." As it is written, "Jacob have I loved, but Esau I have hated."

Ethnic Israel's rejection of the gospel is not an example of God's failure to keep his covenant promises, but of her own failure. Paul clarifies this further by saying that there are and always have been two Israels: those that have been physically descended from Jacob (physical or ethnic Israel) and those who are spiritually descended from him (spiritual Israel or the remnant). Remember back to 2:28–29: "For he is not a Jew who is one outwardly, nor is circumcision that which is outward in the flesh [physical]; but he is a Jew who is one inwardly [spiritual]; and circumcision is that of the heart." Also, 4:11–12 says that Abraham was justified by faith before he was circumcised so that he is the Father of the uncircumcised who believe (gentiles) and the circumcised who walk in the steps of faith (spiritual Israel).

Abraham had two sons, Ishmael and Isaac; it was through Isaac that the promise of salvation would come. God made a sovereign choice that Isaac's line, not Ishmael's, would inherit the covenant promise. God made the decision that the promise would come through Jacob, not Esau. Paul emphasizes that this decision was made before the twins were born and was not based upon any deeds that they had done. He simply chose Jacob and not Esau. We may be thrown off by the language of love and hate, but this is an idiomatic expression for showing preference. Jesus used the same in Luke 14:26 when he said that one cannot be his follower unless he hates his family and his own life (John 12:25). In other words, Jesus must be our preference, our priority, our *numero uno* choice above all. Thus, God preferred or chose Jacob over Esau—not based upon anything in either man (nothing to brag about) but simply according to his own will. Both men were circumcised, but God's promises were fulfilled only through Jacob, spiritual Israel.

2. It is not because God is unjust (vv. 14–18).

> What shall we say then? Is there unrighteousness with God? Certainly not! For He says to Moses, "I will have mercy on whomever I will have mercy, and I will have compassion on whomever I will have compassion." So then it is not of him who wills, nor of him who runs, but of God who shows mercy. For the Scripture says to the Pharaoh, "For this very purpose I have raised you up, that I may show My power in you, and that My name may be declared in all the earth." Therefore He has mercy on whom He wills, and whom He wills He hardens.

Thus, the failure of physical Israel to believe in Christ is not due to God's unfaithfulness, because he did choose a spiritual Israel (a remnant) within physical Israel. However, does this mean that God is unjust to make such a unilateral decision? Certainly not! He will have compassion on whomever he desires. So then, *it* (God's promise of salvation in Christ) *is not of him who wills, nor of him who runs, but of God who shows mercy.* The favor that God showed to Moses (of revealing his Glory) was not due to Moses' just rewards, but simply due to God's mercy. And so the favor he shows to spiritual Israel and not physical Israel is not due to the earned run average of Abraham, Isaac, or Jacob, but simply because God chose to show his mercy. Does that seem unjust? Do you want justice? No, you really don't, because we all deserve condemnation. God's electing grace is not a matter of justice but a matter of mercy.

Let us say that I walk up to my neighbor's house, knock on the door and give her a $100 bill, and then do the same thing for the next three days. Do you think she will be expecting me on the fourth day? I think so. What if I walk past her house to the neighbor next to her, and she comes out and says, "Oh, Dave, I'm home and I am ready for the money." Let's suppose I tell her that I want to give the money to someone else. What if she replies, "But that's not fair!" Would she have a case? No; my giving her the money is not an issue of justice but of mercy. I can give it to whomever I choose.

Paul also says that God's sovereignty is not only demonstrated by showing mercy to those who do not deserve it, but also by hardening the hearts of people who rebel against him. Paul uses the example of Pharaoh who was not made to sin by God, but who was permitted to grow hardened in his sin as a judgment against his rebellion. Paul does not teach a symmetrical view of predestination which says that, on the one hand, God shows mercy and saves some, and on the other hand, he makes people sinful and then condemns them for being sinners. Rather, Paul infers that God shows mercy to some and judges others by permitting a hardening to occur in them due to their own sin. God was not responsible for Pharaoh's sin, but he did punish Pharaoh by hardening his heart and abandoning him to his own stubbornness. Remember that it was Pharaoh who hardened his own heart in the first place (Exod 8:15). This confirmation in rebellion is another way of stating the principle of God's wrath that we see in 1:24, 26, 28: "And God let them go." Leon Morris says, "Neither here nor anywhere else is God said to harden anyone who had not first hardened himself."[1] Why does God harden hearts? . . . "that I may show My power in you, and that My name may be declared in all the earth." Therefore He has mercy on whom He wills, and whom He wills He hardens."

3. It is not because God is unfair (vv. 19–29).

> You will say to me then, "Why does He still find fault? For who has resisted His will?" But indeed, O man, who are you to reply against God? Will the thing formed say to him who formed it, "Why have you made me like this?" Does not the potter have power over the clay, from the same lump to make one vessel for honor and another for dishonor? What if God, wanting to show His wrath and to make His power known, endured with much longsuffering the

1. Morris, *Epistle to the Romans*, 34.

vessels of wrath prepared for destruction, and that He might make known the riches of His glory on the vessels of mercy, which He had prepared beforehand for glory, even us whom He called, not of the Jews only, but also of the Gentiles?

As He says also in Hosea:

"I will call them My people, who were not My people,

And her beloved, who was not beloved."

"And it shall come to pass in the place where it was said to them,

'You are not My people,'

There they shall be called sons of the living God."

Isaiah also cries out concerning Israel:

"Though the number of the children of Israel be as the sand of the sea,

The remnant will be saved.

For He will finish the work and cut it short in righteousness,

Because the Lord will make a short work upon the earth."

And as Isaiah said before:

"Unless the Lord of Sabaoth had left us a seed,

We would have become like Sodom,

And we would have been made like Gomorrah."

Is it fair for God to hold us accountable for our decisions when it seems like he makes all the final decisions? It reminds me of the character Judas in the 1960s rock opera *Jesus Christ Superstar* who criticized God for punishing him when he believed God had chosen him to betray Christ.

First of all, Paul responds by saying that God can do whatever he wants because he has the right of a potter over his clay. Just as it would be unheard of for a lump of clay to ask the potter "Why have you made me into a garbage pot instead of a vase?" so it is inappropriate for us humans to talk back to God. Paul is actually lifting this whole analogy out of Isaiah 29:16 and 45:9–10, using the same audacious and stubborn criticisms of God made by ethnic Israel.

Second, Paul responds by stating in verses 22–24 that we must let God be God. What if God wanted to raise up a Pharaoh (or a Judas) as vessels of wrath and endured their wickedness just to show that he could demonstrate his glory on the vessels of mercy (Moses and Israel)? What if he wanted to do that? What if he wanted to choose some to be saved out of ethnic Israel and the accursed gentile world? What if . . . ? The point is that

God can do whatever he wants and we should not judge his actions by our finite understanding.

Third, Paul responds to the question of why God still finds fault with ethnic Israel. In verses 25–29, Paul simply says it is a part of God's plan, something God said he was going to do. Paul quotes from Hosea 2:23 and 1:10:

> I will call them My people, who were not My people,
> And her beloved, who was not beloved."
> And it shall come to pass in the place where it was said to them,
> "You are not My people,"
>
> There they shall be called sons of the living God.

This is a clear reference to the inclusion of the gentiles, which Peter also makes in 1 Peter 2:10. Paul also quotes from Isaiah 10:20–23 to show that God would raise up a believing remnant (spiritual Israel) from the nation that spurned his covenant: "Isaiah also cries out concerning Israel: "Though the number of the children of Israel be as the sand of the sea, the remnant will be saved."

Keep this concept of the remnant in the back of your mind because it will show that ethnic Israel's rejection is not complete nor is it final. But first, Paul has one more thing to say about Israel's rejection.

B. THE REJECTION OF ETHNIC ISRAEL AND HER REJECTION OF CHRIST (9:30–10)

Review

Paul has explained the unbelief and rejection of ethnic Israel on the basis of God's sovereign decision. Paul has also emphasized that the choice God made to reject a certain part of Israel from being a part of his covenant people was a choice based upon his sovereignty. The reason for such a choice is defended but not explained by Paul and is clarified in a series of four statements explaining the unbelief and rejection of Israel. The first three were covered in the last section:

1. God's rejection of Israel is not because God is unfaithful; it does not invalidate his promises to ancient Israel because he has been faithful to the remnant that he has chosen (vv. 6–13).

2. It is not because God is unjust. God's sovereign choice is not a matter of justice but of mercy. God can have mercy on whomever he pleases (vv. 14–18).

3. It is not because God is unfair (vv. 19–29). What right do we have to talk back to God— like the clay saying to the potter, "Why have you made me like this?" In fact, God's decision to reject national Israel and save a remnant of believing Jews was also a decision of mercy to open the covenant to those who were not God's people, the gentiles.

Preview

We come now to the fourth reason for the rejection of physical Israel: It is because the majority of Israel is proud and has pursued its own righteousness based upon works.

> What shall we say then? That Gentiles, who did not pursue righteousness, have attained to righteousness, even the righteousness of faith; but Israel, pursuing the law of righteousness, has not attained to the law of righteousness. Why? Because they did not seek it by faith, but as it were, by the works of the law. For they stumbled at that stumbling stone. As it is written: "Behold, I lay in Zion a stumbling stone and rock of offense, And whoever believes on Him will not be put to shame." (9:30–33)

Paul makes a transition from the concept of election to the issue of human responsibility. He sets forth a contrast that shows that the grace of God is contrary to human reason. Gentiles, whose self-indulgent lifestyle did not even include a concern for God and his law, have now received righteousness—right-standing with God by faith in Christ. Meanwhile, the majority of Israel who pursued righteousness with religious and moral zeal has fallen short of being right with God. Why? "Because they did not seek it by faith, but as it were, by the works of the law." That doesn't make sense, does it? Those who do not pursue find and those who seek never attain.

The issue is Christ. He is the stumbling (*proskomma*) stone for the Jew. In 1 Corinthians 1:23, Christ crucified is a stumbling block (*skandalon*; the stick or trigger of a trap) to the Jews. In Galatians 5:11, Paul speaks of the offense (*skandalon*) of the cross. Why are Jews scandalized by Christ and the cross? It is because Christ's death on the cross completely undermines their self-righteous reliance upon their ethnicity and the works of the law.

If one could gain a right-standing with God through meritorious works, then the cross and the gospel of Christ would be superfluous. However, if one is saved only by faith in Christ, then good works or ethnicity or cultural superiority are distractions from God's grace.

That is why Paul once again breaks into a passionate plea for his people Israel at the beginning of chapter 10:

> Brethren, my heart's desire and prayer to God for Israel is that they may be saved. For I bear them witness that they have a zeal for God, but not according to knowledge. For they being ignorant of God's righteousness, and seeking to establish their own righteousness, have not submitted to the righteousness of God. For Christ is the end of the law for righteousness to everyone who believes. (vv. 1–4)

Such is true of all religions of self-salvation; there is a zeal for God, but it is not a zeal that leads to the God of grace. Zeal may be admirable, but it is not in itself truth. As we have already said, someone may be sincere, but at the same time sincerely wrong.

> For Moses writes about the righteousness which is of the law, "The man who does those things shall live by them." But the righteousness of faith speaks in this way, "Do not say in your heart, 'Who will ascend into heaven?' (that is, to bring Christ down from above) or, 'Who will descend into the abyss?' (that is, to bring Christ up from the dead). But what does it say? 'The word is near you, in your mouth and in your heart' (that is, the word of faith which we preach)." (vv. 5–8)

Paul lays out two ways of righteousness which are clearly adversarial: that which is by the law and that which is by faith. Each of these ways of righteousness has something to say:

1. Righteousness which is by law—Moses says, "The man who does these things shall live by them" (Lev 18:5). On the surface this seems to mean that keeping the law is a valid way of salvation. However, how do you reconcile that with what Paul says in Galatians 3:10–12? "For as many as are of the works of the law are under the curse; for it is written, 'Cursed is everyone who does not continue in all things which are written in the book of the law, to do them.'" But that no one is justified in the sight of God is evident, for the just shall live by faith. Godet is helpful when he suggests that the law given by God was not given independently of his grace. Salvation was never based upon keeping the law, but upon believing the

promises of God and the provisions of his grace. However, national Israel saw the law as the very way they defined themselves as God's people and as the very means of their salvation. Therefore, they separated law from grace.[2] They took what was meant to reveal sin and used it to achieve their own salvation.

Paul is saying, both here and in Galatians 3, that there is an inherent danger built into the law if it is chosen as a way of righteousness. You must obey it in its entirety or else you are dead. James 2:10 says it more succinctly: "For whoever shall keep the whole law, and yet stumble in one point, he is guilty of all." This is far more than God being extra picky in his demand for righteousness. The very fact that righteousness through the law is so unattainable is proof that it was never meant to be a means of righteousness. Rather, the law was given to me as a mirror to show my unrighteousness and to reveal my need of a savior (Rom 7:7).

2. Righteousness which is by faith- Again Moses is quoted, this time from Deuteronomy 30:12–14: "Do not say in your heart, 'Who will ascend into heaven?' (that is, to bring Christ down from above) or 'Who will descend into the abyss?' (that is, to bring Christ up from the dead)." In other words, our search for salvation is not the result of an Indiana Jones quest for religious knowledge. Paul continues to quote Moses in verse 8, "But what does it say? 'The word is near you, in your mouth and in your heart' (that is, the word of faith which we preach)." The gospel, the way of faith, is attainable by all because Christ has come down from heaven (incarnation) and has come up from out of the abyss (resurrection) so that all the work has been done and is immediately accessible by faith. All one needs to do is "Confess with your mouth the Lord Jesus [incarnation] and believe in your heart that God has raised him from the dead [resurrection], you will be saved. For with the heart one believes unto righteousness, and with the mouth confession is made unto salvation" (vv. 9–10). The gospel is not only attainable to faith, but is also available to all: whoever believes, whether Jew or Greek, whoever calls.

"For the Scripture says, 'Whoever believes on Him will not be put to shame.' For there is no distinction between Jew and Greek, for the same Lord over all is rich to all who call upon Him. For "whoever calls on the name of the Lord shall be saved" (vv. 11–13).

What then is necessary for salvation?

---

2. Godet, *Commentary on Romans*, 377–78.

- Belief in the historical realities about Jesus Christ—his incarnation (that he is God become Man), his death, and resurrection.

- The word of faith (v. 8)—the apostolic gospel which needs to be heard.

- The action of faith—calling upon the name of the Lord to be saved; a decisive event in the heart and demonstrated by a genuine confession (Luke 12:8; John 9:22; 12:42–43).

However, there is one more important component that is missing from the mix, which may come as a complete surprise in the context of the sovereignty of God.

"How then shall they call on Him in whom they have not believed? And how shall they believe in Him of whom they have not heard? And how shall they hear without a preacher? And how shall they preach unless they are sent? As it is written:

'How beautiful are the feet of those who preach the gospel of peace, Who bring glad tidings of good things!' (vv. 14–15).

Notice the progression:

1. How can they call on him in whom they have not believed?

2. And how can they believe in him of whom they have not heard?

3. And how can they hear without a preacher (*kerysso*, "herald")?

4. And how can they preach unless they are sent?

Thus, the missing component to the salvation of an individual is the evangelistic process, consisting of the last two items: someone preaching and someone sending the preacher. So the process of someone coming to faith looks like this:

- Someone is sent.

- Someone preaches.

- Someone hears the preaching.

- The hearer believes.

- The believer calls.

- The caller is saved.

As was mentioned, it is amazing that on the heels of the most specific chapter in the Bible on predestination (Romans 9) follows one of the most forthright chapters on evangelism and missions. It shows us that God's sovereignty and human responsibility must be held together as parallel lines in Scripture. We must preach the gospel because God has ordained the preaching of the gospel to be the very means by which he calls his chosen ones to salvation. In the same way, we must pray; for God has ordained prayer as the means by which he accomplishes his purposes in this world.

What about people who have never heard the gospel? Here are some principles to keep in mind as you struggle with this question:

All are guilty because of Adam's sin (Rom 5:12–19) and our own personal sin (Rom 2:12–16; 3:9–12, 20).

Salvation is only through faith in Jesus Christ (Acts 2:42; Rom 10:9).

All are lost not because they have rejected Christ but because of the guilt of their own sin. (If this were not true then any missionary effort would run the risk of increasing people's condemnation if the message were rejected.)

God has left a witness in every culture (Acts 14:16–17).[3]

There may be some indication that those who have never had the clear light of God's word will not be judged as strictly, but they will still be judged (Luke 12:47–48). When it comes to babies who die and the mentally ill, we trust a God of mercy, and claim Deuteronomy 29:29: "The secret things belong to the Lord our God, but those things which are revealed belong to us and to our children forever."

Paul closes this chapter (vv. 16–21) explaining that the failure of ethnic Israel to respond to the gospel cannot be excused because they did not hear the message or because they could not understand it. He quotes Moses and Isaiah:

"But they have not all obeyed the gospel. For Isaiah says, "LORD, WHO HAS BELIEVED OUR REPORT?" SO THEN FAITH COMES BY HEARING, AND HEARING BY THE WORD OF GOD.

But I say, have they not heard? Yes indeed:

"Their sound has gone out to all the earth,

And their words to the ends of the world."

But I say, did Israel not know? First Moses says:

"I will provoke you to jealousy by those who are not a nation,

I will move you to anger by a foolish nation."

But Isaiah is very bold and says:

"I was found by those who did not seek Me;

3. Richardson, *Eternity in their Hearts*, 25–71.

I was made manifest to those who did not ask for Me."
But to Israel he says:
"All day long I have stretched out My hands
To a disobedient and contrary people."

Israel did not hear the gospel with the ears of faith. Paul implies that hearing the gospel is more than just a physical act. However, there were some in Israel that did hear and were saved. "Faith comes by hearing and hearing by God's word." The implication is that ethnic Israel's lack of hearing was not due to an inability, but to a refusal to hear. They did and do not want to hear the message of Christ because to them it undermines their uniqueness as God's people and destroys their whole system of self-salvation. Additionally, Paul also states that in the face of Israel's rejection of Christ, God has reached out to the gentiles by making the gospel known to them.

Is God finished with ethnic Israel? By no means! God has designed a plan that includes the gentiles in order to make the Jews jealous and angry. Paul will clarify that more in the next chapter. In the meantime, notice the last verse in this chapter which will give us a hint as to what God thinks of ethnic Israel: "All day long I have stretched out my hands to a disobedient and contrary people." In spite of God's election, in spite of Israel's rejection of the gospel, in spite of the rebellion and obstinacy of the Jews, in spite of the gospel being preached to the gentiles, God is not finished with ethnic Israel. Now Paul introduces the concept of the remnant.

C. ISRAEL'S REJECTION IS NOT COMPLETE (11:1–10)

Review

Given the facts that God keeps his promises and that there is nothing that can separate God's people from his love, Paul explains in Romans 9–11 why it seems that God has rejected his covenant people Israel. In chapter 9, Paul says that though a portion of national or ethnic Israel has been rejected by God's sovereign choice, they are not all Israel who are Israel. In other words, God has chosen a portion of Israel, but not *all Israel*. In chapter 10, Paul explains that an immediate cause of ethnic Israel's rejection was their rejection of the gospel of Christ. The gospel is for "all who call upon the name of the Lord" (10:13). Even though Israel has heard the gospel, they have not heard with ears of faith. In chapter 11, Paul comes full circle to explain that the rejection of Israel by God and its rejection of the gospel is neither complete nor is it final. Great hope is held out for the ancient people of God, but it is a hope that will be fulfilled alongside God's plan for the gentiles.

Preview

Paul asks two questions which form the basic structure of this chapter: verse 1: "Has God cast away His people?"; verse 11a: "Have they stumbled that they should fall?" Both address the reasons why ethnic Israel has been rejected and why Israel has rejected the gospel. Both are answered by a resounding "Certainly not!" Both eventually lead to the conclusion that Israel's rejection is neither total nor final.

> I say then, has God cast away His people? Certainly not! For I also am an Israelite, of the seed of Abraham, of the tribe of Benjamin. God has not cast away His people whom He foreknew. Or do you not know what the Scripture says of Elijah, how he pleads with God against Israel, saying, "Lord, they have killed Your prophets and torn down Your altars, and I alone am left, and they seek my life"? But what does the divine response say to him? "I have reserved for Myself seven thousand men who have not bowed the knee to Baal." Even so then, at this present time there is a remnant according to the election of grace. And if by grace, then it is no longer of works; otherwise grace is no longer grace. But if it is of works, it is no longer grace; otherwise work is no longer work. What then? Israel has not obtained what it seeks; but the elect have obtained it, and the rest were blinded. Just as it is written:

> "God has given them a spirit of stupor,
> Eyes that they should not see
> And ears that they should not hear,
> To this very day."
> And David says:
> "Let their table become a snare and a trap,
> A stumbling block and a recompense to them.
> Let their eyes be darkened, so that they do not see,
> And bow down their back always." (vv. 1–10)

Paul gives four reasons to prove that God has not rejected his ethnic Israel:

1. A Personal Reason—"For I am also an Israelite, of the seed of Abraham, of the tribe of Benjamin." The fact that Paul was a believer shows that God has not abandoned his people.   ·

2. A Covenantal Reason—"God has not cast away His people whom He foreknew." The claim is often made that when the Bible says God foreknew someone, it simply means that God knew ahead of time that the person would believe and therefore predestined that person to be saved. John Stott responds by saying that this is not true for two reasons: First of all, God already knows everyone and everything and so foreknowledge must mean something more than knowledge ahead of time. Secondly, if God predestines a person on the basis of foreseen faith, then their salvation is grounded in themselves and in their achievement and not in the free mercy of God.[4] Thus, Paul's understanding of foreknowledge is that a loving choice was made ahead of time ("Jacob have I loved"; 9:13). "You only have I known of all the families of the earth; therefore, I will punish you for all your iniquities" (Amos 3:2). "The Lord did not set his love on you nor choose you because you were more in number than other people, for you were the least of all peoples; but because the Lord loves you, and because he would keep the oath which he swore to your fathers" (Deut 7:7). Schreiner says that foreknowledge implies foreordination because it implies God's covenantal love for his people Israel.[5] John Murray adds that foreknowledge is God's "sovereign, distinguishing love."[6] Thus, in our text, Paul says that it is incomprehensible that God will cast away a people whom he has set his covenantal love upon through an oath to the forefathers.

3. An Historical/Biblical Reason—"Or do you not know what the Scripture says of Elijah, how he pleads with God against Israel, saying, 'Lord, they have killed your prophets and torn down your altars, and I alone am left, and they seek my life'? But what does the divine response say to him? 'I have reserved for myself seven thousand men who have not bowed the knee to Baal.'" Paul calls to our attention the

4. Stott, *Romans*, 249.
5. Schreiner, *Romans*, 580.
6. Murray, *Romans*, 317–18.

historical situation of Israel's apostasy during the days of Ahab and Jezebel. It seemed to Elijah that he alone remained as a believer, but then God revealed that he had preserved a faithful remnant of 7,000 men who had not worshipped Baal.

4. A Contemporary Reason—"Even then at this present time there is a remnant according to the election of grace. And if by grace, then it is no longer of works; otherwise grace is no longer grace. But if it is of works, it is no longer of grace; otherwise work is no longer work." Paul sees the same situation in his day that was true for Elijah; though it seems that the majority of ethnic Israel has rejected the gospel, there exists a significant remnant of those who believe the gospel (Acts 21:20). Thus the existence of a remnant in any age proves that the electing love and grace of God toward Israel has not failed. Paul's mention of grace as opposed to works does not mean that salvation under the Old Covenant was ever based upon works. Schreiner points out that *ouken* (*no longer*) is logical and not temporal.[7] In other words, Paul is emphasizing that election is based on grace and that no one is chosen because of racial or ethnic heritage.

"What then? Israel has not obtained what it seeks; but the elect have obtained it, and the rest were blinded (hardened)." Having already drawn the distinction between national Israel and the believing remnant, Paul continues to speak of this distinction. The majority of the Jews (ethnic Israel) have sought after righteousness, but have not found it because they have tried to establish their own righteousness. However, the minority (the elect or remnant) have obtained righteousness because they received it by faith. The rest (the majority) were hardened because of their rejection of the gospel.

There are three main words for "hardness" in the New Testament: *skleros* ("dry," "rough," "hard"); *porosis* ("callous," "thickened skin," and when used of the eyes, "shortsighted" or "blind"); and *pachyno* ("thick," "fat," "insensitive"). All of these words would be appropriate to describe Israel but Paul uses *porosis* here. I agree with Stott that this hardening or blindness is a judicial punishment that happens to a person or people who continue to reject the gospel and resist God.[8] While God is the agent of hardening, it does not mean that these folks are prevented from finding the truth,

7. Schreiner, *Romans*, 583.

8. Stott, *Romans*, 262–263.

but have become "thick-skinned" in their own blind unbelief because they have rejected the truth. We already discussed this earlier in relationship to Pharaoh, whose heart was hardened by God as he hardened his own heart. This may be a very difficult concept for us to understand and some have erroneously referred to it as double predestination. However, it is important that we should not view it as God electing some to eternal life and some to eternal damnation. Instead, judicial hardening happens when God gives sinners over to unrestrained unbelief, which leads to unrestrained idolatry and immorality, and experiencing the wrath of God in the consequences of their own sin (Rom 1:24, 26, 28).

Paul combines two Old Testament passages to show the pattern of how God gives people over to hardening and blindness after they have rejected the truth (Isa 29:10: Deut 29:4):

> God has given them a spirit of stupor,
> Eyes that they should not see
> And ears that they should not hear,
> to this very day. [Paul adds this last line]

Moses and Isaiah told the Israelites that though they had witnessed the wonders of God, they rejected the Lord. Therefore, in response, God had given them a mind that did not understand; a mind overcome by a spiritual stupor.

Then Paul quotes Psalm 69:22–23:

> Let their table become a snare and a trap,
> A stumbling block and a recompense to them.
> Let their eyes be darkened, so that they do not see,
> And bow down their back always.

This is a difficult verse because Paul interprets it very differently than in its original context. What was originally a curse against the enemies of Israel, Paul now interprets as a curse against the majority of Israel because of their unbelief and rejection of Christ. This very "curse" implies that though God hardens them, that fact does not remove responsibility from the Jews for their unbelief. However, this hardness will not always be there because in the future God will act among ethnic Israel in an unprecedented way. This leads us to our next chapter.

D. ISRAEL'S REJECTION IS NOT FINAL (11:11–36)

Review

In the first section of chapter 11, Paul asks the question "Has God cast away his people"? He answered with a resounding "Certainly not!" and proves his point personally, theologically, biblically, and with a proper understanding that God has chosen a remnant of believing Israel to exist. The rest of national Israel has been blinded or hardened.

Preview

In the second section of chapter 11, Paul asks another question: "Have they stumbled that they should fall?" The word *pesoosin* means to fall utterly and permanently. Again, Paul's response is "Certainly not!" Here we will see that Israel's rejection is neither total nor final.

> I say then, have they stumbled that they should fall? Certainly not! But through their fall, to provoke them to jealousy, salvation has come to the Gentiles. Now if their fall is riches for the world, and their failure riches for the Gentiles, how much more their fullness! (v. 11)

Paul interprets Israel's rejection as something very purposeful. The temporary rejection of ethnic Israel was for the purpose of bringing salvation to the gentiles. Thus when Israel rejected the gospel, "the blessing ricochets from Israel to the Gentiles."[9] We can see this illustrated in the missionary work of Paul where he would first of all go and preach in the synagogue to the Jews. Usually, he would be rejected by the Jews and then he would take the gospel to the gentiles in the same town. In Antioch he said to the Jews, "It was necessary that the word of God was spoken to you first; but since you reject it and judge yourselves unworthy of everlasting life, behold we turn to the Gentiles" (Acts 13:46).[10]

The reaction on the part of the Jews was invariably anger and rage, not a jealousy that would make them want to emulate the faith of the gentiles. However, Paul's mention of jealousy speaks of a future situation and not a

9. Stott, *Romans*, 295.

10. More examples of this pattern; Acts 14:1; 18:5–7; 19:8; 28:28; also Matt 8:10–12; 21:43.

present one. He also adds that if Israel's rejection (fall, loss, defeat) has meant blessing for the gentile world, how much more will (future) Israel's inclusion accrue a much greater blessing for the gentiles. He doesn't explain this right away, but I take this to mean that the worldwide expansion of the gospel will reach its tipping point when ethnic Israel experiences an awakening.

> For I speak to you Gentiles; inasmuch as I am an apostle to the Gentiles, I magnify my ministry, if by any means I may provoke to jealousy those who are my flesh and save some of them. For if their being cast away is the reconciling of the world, what will their acceptance [*pleroma*, "fullness"] be but life from the dead? (vv. 13–15)

These verses parallel verses 11–12 and clarify what he said there. Paul magnifies or glories in (*doxazo*) his ministry to the gentiles, but it is not to the exclusion of the Jews. We have already read of Paul's passionate desire for the salvation of his people. Here we read of his hope to stir his people up to envy so that some of them would be saved. Why does he mention this word *jealousy*? Doesn't it seem an unworthy motive for getting right with God? Jealousy is wrong when we want what someone else has and have no right to it. However, jealousy or envy can be a good motivator if we envy something that is good and is available for all. What if I envy the way a certain husband treats his wife and it makes me want to treat my wife in that same loving way?

Paul desires to make the Jews envious of the gentiles' relationship to God so that they will want it as well. For if Israel's rejection (fall, loss, defeat) meant reconciliation with God for the gentile world, what will the greater blessing of their inclusion or fullness (*pleroma*) mean but "life from the dead." Barrett, Dunn, Cranfield, Kasemann, and Schreiner all understand this as referring to the final resurrection at the close of the Age. A widespread conversion movement within ethnic Israel will trigger the *parousia* ("coming of Christ"), which will be preceded by the general resurrection. Murray leans toward an understanding of life from the dead as newness of life in Christ rather than the resurrection prior to Christ's return. "Life from the dead" (*ek nekron*) is used in two places in the New Testament to refer to spiritual life (Rom 6:13; Eph 5:14), but in most places it means physical resurrection.

Stott believes that it has an analogous meaning signaling a vast and radical revival of religion in the world propelled by national Israel's acceptance of the gospel. This view is held by Calvin, Hodge, Gifford, Godet, and Moule. I also believe this fits best with the parallelism of the text.

> For if the firstfruit is holy, the lump is also holy; and if the root is holy, so are the branches. And if some of the branches were broken off, and you, being a wild olive tree, were grafted in among them, and with them became a partaker of the root and fatness of the olive tree, do not boast against the branches. But if you do boast, remember that you do not support the root, but the root supports you. You will say then, "Branches were broken off that I might be grafted in." Well said. Because of unbelief they were broken off, and you stand by faith. Do not be haughty, but fear. For if God did not spare the natural branches, He may not spare you either. Therefore consider the goodness and severity of God: on those who fell, severity; but toward you, goodness, if you continue in His goodness. Otherwise you also will be cut off. And they also, if they do not continue in unbelief, will be grafted in, for God is able to graft them in again. For if you were cut out of the olive tree which is wild by nature, and were grafted contrary to nature into a cultivated olive tree, how much more will these, who are natural branches, be grafted into their own olive tree? (vv. 16–24)

Paul uses two metaphors and then expands the second one into an allegory. Both of the metaphors illustrate the increasing spread of the influence of ethnic Israel's coming to faith.

1. If the first part of dough offered to God is holy, then the entire "lump" of dough is holy as well. If the believing remnant of the Jews is consecrated to God, the rest is consecrated to him and we can expect their conversion to follow.

2. If the root of the tree is holy, so is the rest of the tree. If the patriarchs are the root of Israel and they are holy, then their descendants (branches) will be holy as well.

Paul goes on to suggest the picture of a cultivated olive tree, which represents the people of God; the root is the patriarchs and the trunk is the continuity of God's covenant down through the centuries. The branches are the people of Israel, the believing remnant and national Israel. The unbelieving Jews in national Israel have been broken off and temporarily discarded while branches from wild olive bushes (representing the gentiles) have been grafted in among the remnant of the Jews. It is important to realize that Paul is describing a picture of the church as "the Israel of God" (Gal 6:16). Lest the gentiles start feeling superior, Paul puts them in their proper place by telling them a few things:

- "You do not support the root but the root supports you." The gentiles have a dependence on the patriarchs and prophets.

- The branches have been broken off to make room for you, but this is no cause for arrogance: "For if God did not spare the natural branches he may not spare you either." You were not naturally a part of the people of God, but you have been grafted in, so your existence is by grace with no reason for boasting.

- "Therefore consider the goodness and severity of God: on those who fell, severity; but toward you, goodness, if you continue in His goodness. Otherwise you also will be cut off." Realize that continuing as the people of God means that you need to continue in the faith (Heb 3:14).

- And if Israel does not persist in her unbelief, then God is able to graft her back into the people of God. After all, this makes much more sense that a natural branch would be grafted in than a branch from a wild olive tree.

> For I do not desire, brethren, that you should be ignorant of this mystery, lest you should be wise in your own opinion, that blindness in part has happened to Israel until the fullness of the Gentiles has come in. And so all Israel will be saved, as it is written:
>
> "The Deliverer will come out of Zion,
> And He will turn away ungodliness from Jacob;
> For this is My covenant with them,
> When I take away their sins." (vv. 25–27)

Paul has now come to a crowning moment—his major point concerning ethnic Israel toward which he has been moving since the beginning of chapter 9. It is the ultimate answer to questions 1 and 2 earlier in chapter 11, showing us that the rejection of Israel is not total or final. Paul calls what he is about to say a *mystery*, not because it is a secret, but because it is about to be revealed: "blindness in part has happened to Israel until the fullness of the Gentiles has come in. And so all Israel will be saved." During the time of this temporary hardening taking place in ethnic Israel, the gospel has continued to go forth and be proclaimed to the ends of the earth. It will continue to be proclaimed "until the fullness (pleroma) of the Gentiles has come in. And so all Israel will be saved."

Many believe that "the full number of Gentiles" and "all Israel" are equivalent phrases both meaning the elect of each group. However, this seems to be importing a concept that is not necessarily in the text itself. In 11:15, the word fullness (*pleroma*) is used to describe the blessing of Israel's future *acceptance* of the gospel. It makes more sense contextually to interpret "the fullness of the Gentiles" not so much in terms of the full number of elect, but in terms of the great numbers of those who will accept the gospel—a great gentile ingathering. Likewise, *all Israel* could refer to a great ingathering of ethnic Israel near the end of human history signaling the return of Christ. This does not mean that every Jewish person will accept Christ, but that belief with be the norm rather than the exception like it seems to be today.[11]

Thus many of the branches of ethnic Israel, which were broken off the olive tree, will be generously grafted back into the people of God. Does this imply, as some believe, that these ethnic Israelites will be saved on the basis of Torah, apart from faith in Christ? Certainly not! This would completely distort Paul's entire message of Romans as well as making him the object of his own curse in Galatians 1 pronounced on those who preached "any other gospel"!

> Concerning the gospel they are enemies for your sake, but concerning the election they are beloved for the sake of the fathers. For the gifts and the calling of God are irrevocable. For as you were once disobedient to God, yet have now obtained mercy through their disobedience, even so these also have now been disobedient, that through the mercy shown you they also may obtain mercy. For God has committed them all to disobedience, that He might have mercy on all. (vv. 28–32)

Paul summarizes his thought in verses 28–32 with a very interesting series of dialectical statements:

- Ethnic Israel is at the same time enemies of the gospel and loved by God because they were chosen by him (God's call is irrevocable).

- You gentiles were at one time disobedient, but now have received mercy through Israel's disobedience.

- So Israel, which is now disobedient, will also receive mercy through the same mercy shown you.

11. See Appendix One for a more complete comparison of the major views on how to interpret "all Israel will be saved."

- God has bound all (*tous pantas*) people over to disobedience so that he might have mercy on them all.

This quote by Thomas Schreiner summarizes Paul's overall thought in this chapter:

> Israel has been temporarily hardened while the Gentiles stream into the church. But at the end of history all Israel will be saved. Israel's eschatological (end times) salvation will occur . . . and will fulfill God's irrevocable covenant promises to his people. God has planned history in such a way that his mercy is featured. In the current era he showers his blessings upon Gentiles, who have long opposed him. In the future, he will turn his merciful eye toward Israel, which resists him while Gentiles enter the people of God. God's plan in history was to confine all under disobedience, so that he might show his mercy to both Jews and Gentiles in a more stunning way.[12]

Paul concludes with an expression of praise and adoration for the wisdom and knowledge of God.

> Oh, the depth of the riches both of the wisdom and knowledge of God! How unsearchable are His judgments and His ways past finding out!
> "For who has known the mind of the Lord?
> Or who has become His counselor?"
> "Or who has first given to Him
> And it shall be repaid to him?"
> For of Him and through Him and to Him are all things, to whom be glory forever. Amen. (vv. 33–36)

John Stott reminds us of something strategically important about our faith:

> Theology (our belief about God) and doxology (our worship of God) should never be separated. On the one hand, there can be no doxology without theology. It is not possible to worship an unknown god . . . On the other hand, there should be no theology without doxology. There is something fundamentally flawed about a purely academic interest in God. . . . Our places are on our faces before him.[13]

To God be the Glory!

12. Schreiner, *Romans*, 591.
13. Stott, *Romans*, 32.

PART TWO

Chapters 12–16

I

God's Grace Expressed in the Life of the Believing Community (12:1—15:13)

A. IN A LIFE OF CONSECRATION (12:1-2)

Review

PAUL BEGINS THIS SECTION *I appeal to you therefore* (*oun*); also translated *now, so then*, or *consequently*. This very word throws us back to what Paul has already said about the mercy of God being shown to both the "grafted-in" gentiles and those temporarily hardened among ethnic Israel (11:30–32), as well as God's merciful dealings with sinful and enslaved humanity through justification by faith (chapters 1–5).

Preview

A true understanding of the mercies of God in Christ will motivate us to present our bodies for his service, which will yield a life characterized by worship. Such an offering of ourselves will cause us to distance ourselves from the thoughts, values, and behaviors of this present age, and experience a progressive transformation of character. This change will be realized as our minds are renewed by God's word and our behavior is patterned after God's will.

"I appeal to you therefore, brothers, by the mercies of God." Paul does not use his Apostolic position to command the church, nor does he use guilt to motivate. Instead he implores or urges his fellow believers to do something and motivates them by the variegated and deep mercies of God. It is not our baptism that saves; not our catechism, first communion, our church-going or generosity—but the mercies of God in Christ alone. Thus it is for those of us who have received such mercies that Paul frames his appeal.

"Present your bodies as a living sacrifice." Paul urges his brothers to *present (paristimi)*, to offer, to place at the disposal of God—*your bodies*. Some translations have "yourselves" but the Greek word is *somata*, "bodies." There was a heresy beginning in Paul's day which claimed that the physical body was evil and the spiritual was good. However, Paul taught that our bodies are external manifestations of who we are, and if our hearts have been captured by the mercies of God, our eyes, mouths, hands, and feet should be captured as well. And so we are to place everything we are at the disposal of the merciful God who saved us by his grace. "Do not, then, allow sin to establish any power over your mortal bodies in making you give way to your lusts. Nor hand over your organs to be, as it were, weapons of evil for the devil's purposes" (Rom 6:12–13, Phillips). We can infer then that we are a living sacrifice, not a dead one; we are a holy sacrifice, not an unholy one; we are an acceptable and well-pleasing sacrifice to God, not one that strives to curry favor. But there's more. . . .

"Holy and acceptable which is your spiritual ["rational," "reasonable"] worship." Offering our bodies to God is an act of worship. This is not worship done in a church or temple service, but worship done through our bodies which are called the temples of the Holy Spirit—the worship through one's work, study, care for the poor and needy, teaching and training of the young. The word for "spiritual" could be translated as "reasonable" (*logikos*—1 Pet 2:2); not something mechanical where we just go through the motions. However, the concept of reasonable worship can also mean that a failure to yield ourselves to God, who has been so merciful, is the height of folly and irrationality.[1] A clearer definition of what it means to offer your body to God is "fleshed out" in the next verse.

"Do not be conformed to this world." The word for "conform" (*suschematizo*) is where we get the word "scheme" ("pattern"). Presenting our bodies to God means that we will not allow ourselves to be molded by the world's schemes—its values, behavior, and ambitions.

The following is an illustration from the movie *Zelig*, starring and directed by Woody Allen. It is a mockumentary whose scenes are made to look like vintage newsreel clips from the 1920s and 1930s. The main character is Leonard Zelig, a man who reflected the prevailing relativism of his age. In his mind, he became whomever he was with and even began to evidence their physical characteristics; whether overweight, Asian, African, female, etc. He was a human chameleon. Ultimately, Zelig was institutionalized, went through psycho-therapy and learned to resist the urge to conform by saying "no" to whatever was said. He ended up so disagreeable that he was institutionalized for being anti-social.

Too many of us are Zelig Christians—becoming like whoever we are around. This reminds me of my high school days when I would sit in the back of the bus on wrestling trips where all the dirty stories were being told. In my heart, I knew I did not belong there, but outwardly I wanted to belong and so I conformed. "For I do not do the good I want, but the evil I do not want is what I keep on doing" (Rom 7:19). However, Paul said that the ultimate definition of offering myself to God is to . . .

"But be transformed . . ." The word "transform" is the word for "metamorphosis" (*metamorphoo*). The word is translated in Matthew 17:2 as "transfigured"—such as when Jesus was transformed before the very eyes of his disciples and they saw his real glory, not just his outward form. And so Paul tells us to let "the real you" come out.

When I hear the word "metamorphosis" I think of the process of a tadpole becoming a beautiful frog. (Yes, I think they are beautiful!) Depending on the species, this process lasts from two weeks to two months. A gradual change takes place whereby this tadpole-with-a-frog nature begins to actually look like a frog and not a fish. It absorbs its tail; its intestines shorten; its back legs, then front legs, grow out. Finally, its gills become lungs so it cannot breathe in its original environment. And if the frog continues to think it is a tadpole, it is in for severe consequences.

---

1. Schreiner, *Romans*, 645.

The frog does not create this change itself. It happens though the laws of nature, which God established at Creation. Likewise, our spiritual transformation is a process accomplished in us by God through the work of his Holy Spirit and . . .

". . . by the renewal of your mind." This newness of mind does not refer to a brain transplant, but to a new capacity to understand things we have never before understood. Perhaps this is what Paul meant when he said, "Now we have received not the spirit of the world, but the Spirit who is from God, that we might understand the things freely given to us by God" (1 Cor 2:12). In Romans 1:18–32, Paul spoke about the darkened and futile thinking that characterized those alienated from God, free-falling into a downward spiral of moral and behavioral depravity.

However, because of God's mercies, the pattern is reversed and we receive a new ability to grow in understanding, thinking, and processing the truth of God's word. "Blessed is the man who walks not in the counsel of the wicked, nor stands in the way of sinners, nor sits in the seat of scoffers; but his delight is in the law of the Lord, and on his law he meditates day and night" (Ps 1:1–2). This new way of thinking is based upon God's word and sets in motion a metamorphosis of character which desires to "mortify the flesh"; no longer seeking to conform itself to the counsel and ways of the world, but to the will of God.

". . . that by testing you may discern what is the will of God, what is good and acceptable and perfect." The result of a renewed mind is the ability to discern God's will. We struggle with the concept of knowing the will of God. Whom should we marry? Should we go to college or into the trades? When will we get a new job? Who will be our new pastor? We find it frustrating because we often think that God's will is a body of data that must be accessed rather than a relationship that must be developed.

Let me illustrate it with the story of the little boy who wanted to go outside to play even though it was getting close to suppertime. His mom gave him permission, but he had to agree to stay around the house so he could hear her call. Happily he went outside and saw a buddy just across the street. Then they saw another friend down at the end of the street. He wasn't even thinking that he had moved out of earshot of the house. Soon his stomach began to growl and he noticed it was getting dark, so he ran home and saw that supper was over and the dishes already washed. He was sent to bed without supper, not because he didn't hear his mom call (that was his excuse), but because he did not stay around the house.

It could be that we are so busy living the way we want to live that when we suddenly get hungry to know God's will, we cannot hear his voice. The reason is not that God is being secretive, but that we are not "around the house" to hear him speak. Paul does not give us a formula for knowing God's will, but he does give us a surefire way of staying attuned to him.

- On the basis of the mercy that has been shown to you in Christ, offer your whole being to him and let every part of your life be an act of worship to the One who gave himself for you.

- Your life of worship will be fleshed out by nonconformity to the world and by being transformed as you use your renewed mind to know him more and strive to understand his truth found in Scripture.

- Then you will be able to discern his will, because you will know what pleases him and live accordingly on a daily basis and not just when you have a big decision to make.

B. IN A HUMBLE AND CARING MINISTRY WITHIN THE CHURCH (12:3-21)

Review

The life that pleases God is the life that is surrendered to God; the self-surrendered life. Paul began Romans 12 by urging his brothers and sisters in Rome, in view of the mercies of God, to offer their bodies to God as a living, holy, and acceptable sacrifice. Such an action is not only reasonable, but is also the very basis of a transformed life through the renewal of the mind—an entirely new way of thinking based upon God's word.

Preview

Paul now continues in 12:3–21 to show how the self-surrendered life works itself out in relationship to others, which is the subject matter of the rest of the book. It is about others: people we like and those we don't; people who agree with us and those who don't; people inside the church and those on the outside.

This text helps us answer the question: What will the life of self-surrender look like? This passage breaks down into three basic characteristics:

1. A Humble and Realistic View of our Spiritual Gifts (vv. 3–8).

> For by the grace given to me I say to everyone among you not to think of himself more highly than he ought to think, but to think with sober judgment, each according to the measure of faith that God has assigned. For as in one body we have many members, and the members do not all have the same function, so we, though many, are one body in Christ, and individually members one of another. Having gifts that differ according to the grace given to us, let us use them: if prophecy, in proportion to our faith; if service, in our serving; the one who teaches, in his teaching; the one who exhorts, in his exhortation; the one who contributes, in generosity; the one who leads, with zeal; the one who does acts of mercy, with cheerfulness.

Spiritual gifts are the special abilities, which God gives to each person when she or he becomes a believer. These gifts are not to be confused with natural talents or learned abilities. For example, you may have a career in teaching, but teaching may not be your spiritual gift. These gifts (lit. *charismata*, "grace-gifts") are the direct result of the grace of God in our lives. God not only saves us, but also equips us to serve others in the church by means of the individualized expressions of the Holy Spirit in the life of each believer.

Therefore, the answer to where we should serve is found in the answer to what is our gift? In verses 6–8, Paul gives a partial list: prophecy, service, teaching, encouragement (exhortation), giving, leadership/administration, and mercy. If we combine this list with other gifts mentioned in other places (1 Cor 12; Eph 4; 1 Pet 4), we could come up with a list of close to twenty-five. One way to determine your gift is by asking another believer who knows you pretty well and has seen you serve. My Young Life regional director was the one who pointed out my gifting after he saw me in action with my Young Life Club. Another way to determine your gift is by taking a gifts inventory.[2]

---

2. Here are some excellent online sites, which offer free inventories that you might find helpful: https://www.lifeway.com/en/articles/women-leadership-spiritual-gifts-growth -service. http://www.churchgrowth.org/cgi-cg/gifts.cgi?intro=1 http://www.buildingchurch .net/g2s.htm.

Paul's main concern in our text is how we should exercise these gifts once we know them. "I say to everyone among you is not to think of himself more highly than he ought to think, but to think with sober judgment, each according to the measure of faith that God has assigned." The Greek word for "to think" (*fronein*) shows up four times in verse 3. Your English version shows three, but the word translated as a phrase "to think with sober judgment" (*sofronein*) is the fourth. It means to have realistic thoughts about the gift(s) you have been given. Some people may be prone to think too highly of themselves because their gifts are more high-profile and may bring a certain amount of accolade. Others may feel that they are not very important to the work of God because they are behind-the-scenes people and their gifts are not as noticeable.

For both the high and low profile giftedness, Paul tells us to be realistic in our thinking because whatever has been given to us is for the common good. Our gifts are not as much about us as about their usefulness to others. For those of you who have the gifts of mercy, service, and encouragement, you are the backbone of the church—serving quietly without much fanfare. Do not think you are unimportant even though you may be unnoticed. God has shown you mercy and has gifted you to do the same in his body.

And for those of you with a high profile gift, it is not about you. Whatever has been given to you is not so that you can attract attention to yourself, but so that you can draw others' attention to God. For those with gifts of preaching, teaching, and leadership—though you are the face of the church, serving out in front for all to see—do not think you are essential. Remember that God used a donkey in the Old Testament to speak his word. And the only star he used to lead people to Jesus was the star of Bethlehem! God has shown you mercy and has positioned you in his body to do the same.

Be aware that spiritual pride can also parade itself as humility. I heard a story told about a pastor and his experience with a very accomplished musician in his new church. John had played a beautiful offertory on the piano and the pastor thanked him for it after the service. John's reply was, "It wasn't me; it was the Lord." A few weeks later, the same thing happened and John replied the same way. This bothered the pastor. Finally, it happened again and after John replied, "It wasn't me; it was the Lord," the pastor came back with "Come on, John, you and I both know that the Lord can play better than that!"

2. A Genuine and Active Love for Other Believers (vv. 9–18).

> Let love be genuine. Abhor what is evil; hold fast to what is good. Love one another with brotherly affection. Outdo one another in showing honor. Do not be slothful in zeal, be fervent in spirit, serve the Lord. Rejoice in hope, be patient in tribulation, be constant in prayer. Contribute to the needs of the saints and seek to show hospitality. Bless those who persecute you; bless and do not curse them. Rejoice with those who rejoice, weep with those who weep. Live in harmony with one another. Do not be haughty, but associate with the lowly. Never be wise in your own sight. Repay no one evil for evil, but give thought to do what is honorable in the sight of all. If possible, so far as it depends on you, live peaceably with all.

"Let love be genuine." The word for "genuine" is *anupokritos* which means "without hypocrisy" or literally "without a mask." In the Greek theatre there were no backgrounds, scenery, or costumes, and only a few actors who would play multiple parts. Thus, every actor would carry a mask or two which he would hold over his face when he wanted to portray a particular character. Our love for one another should not be like speaking out from under a mask. It should not be play-acting, but real, sincere, and characterized by actions. In verses 9–14 we see this call to sincere and active love in our church relationships laid out in couplets:

"Abhor (*apostugeo*, "loathe") what is evil in one another; *hold fast* (*kalleo*, "glued together") to what is good." We need to be discerning in our relationships, wanting the best for each other.

"*Love* (*philostorgos*, "natural affection") one another *with brotherly affection* (*philadelphia*, "tender affection"). Outdo each other in showing honor." Only compete with each other to see who show more respect.

"Do not be slothful in zeal, *be fervent* (on fire) in spirit, serve the Lord." Do not get lazy, but be enthusiastic about Jesus and about one another.

"Rejoice in hope, be patient in tribulation, be constant in prayer." If you like triplets, check this one out! How do you think they are connected?

"Contribute to the needs of the saints" (be generous). The word *contribute* is more than just putting money in the offering. It means to share and is the verb *koinonoe* from which we get the word "fellowship"; "and seek to show hospitality" (*philoxenia*, "love of the stranger"), not just love of the brother.

"Bless those you persecute you; bless and do not curse them." Show good will toward those who don't like you. This is a unique twist of the

Golden Rule: do unto our enemies exactly the opposite of what they do to you.

"Rejoice with those who rejoice; weep with those who weep." Do not stand aloof from others so that you are unaffected by their joy or sorrow.

"Live in harmony with one another and do not be haughty but associate with the lowly": Literally, "be of the same mind with one another" (Phil 2:2). This does not mean agreement on every issue, but having a mind set on the same purpose and end, along with an attitude of humility—note the contrast between like-minded and high-minded or condescending.

"Repay no one evil for evil, but give thought to do what is honorable in the sight of all." Yes, evil words and actions occur even within the church and our reaction is to pay them back in the same currency. However, we are told to deal honorably even with those who have hurt us deeply. Pastors especially should take note of this. You cannot act toward others as they act toward you. The damage you might do to one of your stubborn sheep would be incalculable.

"If possible, so far as it depends on you, live peaceably with all." Living peaceably with some people may not be possible, but love means that the hindrance should never come from us. We must strive, as far as possible, to be reconciled to all within the body of Christ.

3. A Missional Approach to Those Who Oppose Us (vv. 19–21).

"Beloved, never avenge yourselves, but leave it to the wrath of God, for it is written, "Vengeance is mine, I will repay," says the Lord. To the contrary, "If your enemy is hungry, feed him; if he is thirsty, give him something to drink; for by so doing you will heap burning coals on his head. Do not be overcome by evil, but overcome evil with good."

I believe that Paul now looks at how the self-surrendered servant behaves outside the church in a world that may be hostile to the gospel. Does he mean that the Christian should never defends himself or never desires justice for himself? I do not think that is his point. In the book of Acts we see where Paul himself sought protection and justice from mistreatment and persecution on three different occasions, using the shield of his Roman citizenship complete with the rights and protection that came with it.

Instead, I think Paul is speaking of those situations in which the self-surrendered servant of God is abused and wronged, and where the natural tendency is to fight back and retaliate. At those times, the believer should think and act with a missional purpose so that if an enemy is hungry or thirsty, he should be fed and given something to drink. Paul is advocating a similar response as in verses 17 and 19: "repay no one evil for evil . . . you will heap burning coals upon his head."

What does that mean? Some people believe that these *burning coals* represent judgment based upon the fact that the metaphor is never used in a positive sense in the Old Testament (2 Sam 22:9; Pss 11:6; 18:8, 12; 140:10; Prov 6:27–29; Ezek 24:11). Thus they would say that our kind actions are a beneficent revenge increasing the guilt of an evil person: be kind to your enemy so he will really get "burned" in the day of judgment.

However, I think Paul's response reflects the missional purpose of his life and is more in keeping with the theme of self-surrender in this text. Also, it is important to notice that the burning coals are not a reference to God's action, but to our action as believers.[3] Repaying vengeance is God's action; heaping the burning coals on the head of our enemy is our responsibility. The two should not be confused. Let me give you an interpretation of "heap burning coals on the head" which comes from an Indian Christian, Bishop K. C. Pillai.[4]

Pillai describes growing up fatherless in a small village in India. His single mother supported the family by selling burning embers of charcoal from which people could start their fires in the morning. The writer remembers during winter, after his mother had risen before dawn and had the charcoal glowing, she would awaken him so he could deliver them to the neighbors in the village. It was so cold and he would be shivering. His mother would place several pieces of charcoal in a bowl-shaped shard of pottery. The boy would then put the bowl on his head in order to carry the coals. As he went, he distinctly remembers that the burning coals on his head would gradually warm up his entire body. Pillai interprets what Paul is saying from this perspective; by overcoming evil with good, we may warm up our enemies to the gospel.

See how the gospel changes everything? Our relationships in the church and in the world will never be the same because we have been changed into people surrendered to God. Do you use your gifts so that others will be helped and God will be glorified? Do you love the brothers and sisters sincerely and genuinely, doing everything within your power to live reconciled? Do you desire to do good to those who persecute and oppose

3. Schreiner, *Romans*, 675.
4. Pillai, *Eastern Window*, 45.

you, so that they will see the gospel lived out and be warmed to it? If not, then "I appeal to you therefore, brothers, by the mercies of God, to present your bodies as a living sacrifice . . ."

C. IN THE REALITIES OF POLITICAL AND SOCIAL LIFE (13:1–7)

Review

There are three relational environments in which we are to live our lives as self-surrendered servants. As those who have been objects of God's great mercy and love, we are to give ourselves completely to God; we are to love and strive to be intentionally reconciled to those in the body of Christ; and we are to live in a missional relationship with our enemies.

Preview

We come now to the fourth key relationship of the Christian, which is to the governing authorities of the state. This is arguably a very difficult passage to interpret to the satisfaction of many; therefore, I will do the best I can to draw out some basic principles from it and two other related biblical passages.

> Let every person be subject to the governing authorities. For there is no authority except from God, and those that exist have been instituted by God. Therefore whoever resists the authorities resists what God has appointed, and those who resist will incur judgment. For rulers are not a terror to good conduct, but to bad. Would you have no fear of the one who is in authority? Then do what is good, and you will receive his approval, for he is God's servant for your good. But if you do wrong, be afraid, for he does not bear the sword in vain. For he is the servant of God, an avenger who carries out God's wrath on the wrongdoer. Therefore one must be in subjection, not only to avoid God's wrath but also for the sake of conscience. For because of this you also pay taxes, for the authorities are ministers of God, attending to this very thing. Pay to all what is owed to them: taxes to whom taxes are owed, revenue to whom revenue is owed, respect to whom respect is owed, honor to whom honor is owed. (vv. 1–7)

Once again it should be noted that this passage is set in the larger context that challenges the Christian to define him/herself by submission, reconciliation, and kindness even to the enemy. "Bless those who persecute you . . . do not repay evil for evil . . . do not take revenge but leave room for God's wrath, for it is written, 'Vengeance is mine, I will repay,' says the Lord" (Rom 12:19). Paul sets out our duty as individual Christians to neither avenge ourselves nor defend ourselves from those who try to do us harm. This mirrors the words of Jesus in Matthew 5:38–39: "You have heard that it was said, 'eye for eye, and tooth for tooth.' But I tell you, do not resist an evil person. If someone strikes you on the right cheek, turn to him the other also" (NIV).

"An eye for an eye," known as the *lex talionis* (Exod 21:24), was a law set down by God that governed retribution by a legitimate authority for a crime. If you poked someone's eye out, the authorities were permitted and limited to poking out only one of your eyes, not both of them. If you killed someone premeditatedly, the authorities could take only your life and not the lives of your children. Jesus says that we do not have the right to exercise this kind of retribution in our personal relationships, and Paul says in Romans 12 that we must leave such retribution in the hands of God. And what does God use to accomplish this justice? He uses governing authorities.

Thus, civil authority has been established by God and has been given the power of the sword (the New Testament version of *lex talionis*) to punish evildoers. Whoever rebels against this authority rebels against God. Therefore, the retribution that we are prohibited from taking on a personal level, the state can take in the interest of maintaining a just and orderly society.

What then is our responsibility to the state, according to Romans 13?

- Submit ourselves to governing authorities not merely out of fear, but also out of conscience—because it is the right thing to do (13:5). It is important to recognize that Paul's frame of reference was not a Republican or Democratic president, but Nero, who hated Christians and who eventually used the power of the sword to take the very life of the apostle Paul. Most of us have never had to submit to this kind of authority.

- Pay our taxes (13:7) because this helps God's servants (lit. "minister," *leitourgos*—always denotes religious or priestly service) to carry out their function of ruling, protecting, and pursuing justice.

- Give the state whatever is its due: taxes, revenue (tolls), respect, honor. We find here a vague reference to Matthew 22:21: "Render to Caesar what is Caesar's, and to God the things that are God's."

Let's look at another passage by another apostle and see if there are similarities: 1 Peter 2:13–17. "Be subject for the Lord's sake to every human institution, whether it be to the emperor as supreme, or to governors as sent by him to punish those who do evil and to praise those who do good. For this is the will of God, that by doing good you should put to silence the ignorance of foolish people. Live as people who are free, not using your freedom as a cover-up for evil, but living as servants of God. Honor everyone. Love the brotherhood. Fear God. Honor the emperor."

- Submit yourselves to those in authority for the Lord's sake. On the one hand, such obedience glorifies the Lord Jesus (Colossians 3:23) and on the other hand, such obedience commends the gospel to our culture. Peter's concern is that a rebellious attitude toward civil authority could bring reproach to the name of Christ (v.15).

- Submit yourselves in freedom. We make a conscious choice to submit ourselves in order to show we are the servants of God. Though we are citizens of God's Kingdom, we freely choose to submit ourselves to the government under which we live. We are Christians first and Americans, Nigerians, Greeks, Russians, Polish, French, Irish, etc., second. Our primary allegiance is to Christ's Kingdom.

- Show proper respect to everyone, whether they be in the church or in the world; whether "Average Joes" or those high up in government like the president. Though we disagree with those in power, we are to show respect. We do not need to like the person in authority; we are to honor him or her. Once again, let's remember that Peter is referring to Nero, who would be the one to take his life.

There is one final passage written by Paul on this subject found in his counsel to Timothy in 1 Timothy 2:1–4. "First of all, then, I urge that supplications, prayers, intercessions, and thanksgivings be made for all people, for kings and all who are in high positions, that we may lead a peaceful and quiet life, godly and dignified in every way. This is good, and it is pleasing in the sight of God our Savior, who desires all people to be saved and to come to the knowledge of the truth."

- Pray for those in authority. This is a priority. It is the first thing that Paul urges Timothy to teach his flock. Notice the various kinds of prayers mentioned— requests, prayers, intercession, and thanksgiving. These are not differences in technique, but in comprehensiveness. God told Jeremiah to tell those taken into captivity in Babylon, "Seek the welfare of the city to which I have sent you into exile, and pray to the Lord on its behalf, for in its welfare you will find welfare" (Jeremiah 29:7). The prophet was commanded to pray for the nation that was holding him and his people in captivity. What should we pray for when we pray for our rulers? John Calvin gives us one insight: "Thus we should not only pray for those who are already worthy, but we must pray to God that he might make bad men good."[5]

- Pray also that our rulers may fulfill their God-given function of maintaining order and peace. However, our ultimate concern for peace is so that the gospel will go forth unhindered.

In summary: these are the bottom-line principles from Romans 13 upon which we Christians can agree:

- Submit to authority
- Recognize that the government has the power of the sword
- Give to the government what is the government's due
- Respect our rulers
- Pray for our rulers
- Though citizens of heaven, seek peace for the country of our earthly citizenship

However, in spite of these common principles there are two very different perspectives that Christians hold. The first is what we call *pacifism*. Since the Christian is a part of the kingdom of God characterized by peace and reconciliation, s/he can have no involvement with the secular authority of the state since it has been empowered to take life. For the Christian to intentionally take another person's life is always wrong. Since war is killing people *en masse*, war is also always wrong.

In addition, for many pacifists a Christian cannot hold public office, be involved in any kind of law enforcement, or be in the military. Christians are to see themselves as a part of a global community especially concerned

5. Calvin, *Commentary on 1 Timothy*, 52.

with using their influence in issues of poverty and injustice, peace and reconciliation, and not war and violence. Evil can be overcome only with good. Physical force is always an ungodly solution to conflict, and it never accomplishes the lasting purposes of God. War breeds more war. All the ethical prescriptions of the Sermon on the Mount (especially Matthew 5:39–41) are not merely for the individual but also for a national ethic. The church should have a prophetic role that holds government accountable to this ethic.

However, there are several streams that flow out of the pacifist position. Perhaps you have read the book or seen the movie about Desmond Doss, the "Hero of Hacksaw Ridge." Doss was a Seventh-Day Adventist who believed that bearing arms in any war would break the sixth commandment prohibiting the taking of human life. He became a conscientious objector, but enlisted and served as a Medic in the seventy-seventh infantry division during World War II and single-handedly saved about a hundred soldiers' lives on Okinawa. He refused to carry a weapon because of his convictions, but called himself a "conscientious cooperator" instead of a conscientious objector. He defended his position this way to a fellow soldier who accused him of enjoying the benefits of religious freedom while not shouldering any of its responsibility:

> "That's where you're wrong, sergeant," Desmond said earnestly. "In my church we're taught to obey government authority, just like the Bible says. You'll never find me failing to salute the flag or trying to get out of a detail. I love this country as much as you do."[6]

The second perspective on the Christian's relationship to government is what we will call *activism*. This belief holds that since God has ordained government, Christians are in the best position to be involved in government since they understand its proper function. What is forbidden to individuals, the power of retribution and punishment, is given to the government in the "power of the sword." Therefore, it is appropriate for government (and for Christians involved in government) to take life when it is for a just cause or when it is to protect society from a greater evil. The sixth commandment is "Thou shall not murder," not "Thou shall not kill." This means that the power of taking life has been given to the state for use in capital punishment (Gen 9:5–6), law enforcement, and in war. Certainly government often carries these out in unjust ways, but activists believe the Bible makes it clear that government has the authority for these actions.

---

6. Herndon, *Hacksaw Ridge*, 15.

PART TWO

In addition, activism does not mean a mindless obedience to the state. Acts 4:18–31 and 5:17–29 exemplify the need for civil disobedience when a government forbids what God requires or requires what God forbids.

> But as soon as governors lead us away from obedience to God, seeing that they enter into conflict with God impiously and boldly, they must be put in their place, so that God's authority may stand supreme. Then all the fumes of their offices will vanish. For God does not think men worthy of titles of honor in order that they obscure His own glory . . . If a king or a prince or a magistrate extols himself so much that he minimizes to honor the authority of God, he is nothing but a man.[7]

Nuremberg and My Lai have taught us that blind obedience to unjust commands do not relieve an individual of personal responsibility. Christians have a prophetic responsibility to hold the state accountable for its actions and policies based on Scripture. I believe Christians should also work for policy change, vote for candidates of character, and urge government to fulfill its proper role to rule, protect, and keep order. We should do this with honor and respect, and never stoop to the disrespectful, politicized hostility towards authority often demonstrated by many modern protest movements. Such activism considers it essential to be respectful of authority because we do not want to bring reproach to the cause of Christ and we desire to follow in his footsteps (1 Pet 2:21).

Two questions could be asked at this point: Under what circumstances should a Christian refuse to obey a ruling authority? Look at the examples of the Hebrew midwives (Exod 1:15–19); Shadrach, Meshach, and Abednego's refusal to bow down to Nebuchadnezzar's statue (Dan 3:4–18); Daniel's disobedience of the king's order not to pray (Dan 6:6–16); and Peter and John's two-time refusal to stop preaching in the name of Jesus (Acts 4:19; 5:29). It should be noted that in each of these cases the individuals disobeyed, but they remained submitted to the ruling authority. Civil disobedience does not seek to overthrow ruling authority, but to prophetically call that authority to account for an immoral or unjust law or practice. Thus the Christian should live in obedience to a ruling authority unless that authority violates the law of God.

Martin Luther King held a similar perspective and gave an explanation of it in a letter he wrote in April, 1963, from a jail cell in Birmingham, Alabama, to a group of clergy who believed his civil rights protests were

---

7. Harrison et al., *Christian and the State*, 26.

"untimely" and against the law. The following is a portion of that letter and, though lengthy, I include it because of its relevance to our discussion of the activist interpretation of Romans 13:1–7:

> You express a great deal of anxiety over our willingness to break laws. This is certainly a legitimate concern. . . . One may well ask: "How can you advocate breaking some laws and obeying others?" The answer lies in the fact that there are two types of laws: just and unjust. I would be the first to advocate obeying just laws. One has not only a legal but a moral responsibility to obey just laws. Conversely, one has a moral responsibility to disobey unjust laws. I would agree with St. Augustine that "an unjust law is no law at all."
>
> Now, what is the difference between the two? How does one determine whether a law is just or unjust? A just law is a man-made code that squares with the moral law or the law of God. An unjust law is a code that is out of harmony with the moral law. To put it in the terms of Saint Thomas Aquinas: "An unjust law is a human law that is not rooted in eternal law and natural law." Any law that uplifts human personality is just. Any law that degrades human personality is unjust. All segregation statutes are unjust because segregation distorts the soul and damages the personality. . . . Hence segregation is not only politically, economically and sociologically unsound, it is morally wrong and sinful. . . . Thus it is that I can urge men to obey the 1954 decision of the Supreme Court, for it is morally right; and I can urge them to disobey segregation ordinances, for they are morally wrong."
>
> Sometimes a law is just on its face and unjust in its application. For instance, I have been arrested on a charge of parading without a permit. Now, there is nothing wrong in having an ordinance which requires a permit for a parade. But such an ordinance becomes unjust when it is used to maintain segregation and to deny citizens the First-Amendment privilege of peaceful assembly and protest. . . . In no sense do I advocate evading or defying the law, as would the rabid segregationist. That would lead to anarchy. One who breaks an unjust law must do so openly, lovingly, and with a willingness to accept the penalty. I submit that an individual who breaks a law that conscience tells him is unjust, and who willingly accepts the penalty of imprisonment in order to arouse the conscience of the community over its injustice, is in reality expressing the highest respect for law.[8]

---

8. King, *Letter*, para. 13–17.

The second question that could be asked is, would there ever be a time when Christians could participate in the overthrow of a governing authority? Consider our own American Revolution. Many Christians and pastors called for rebellion against the tyranny of the British government. They insisted that English rule did not reflect the authority of God nor the consent of those ruled and therefore it should be overthrown. What would you have done?

An example that shows the agony of this question regarding the overthrow of government is found in the life of Dietrich Bonhoeffer, a German theologian and pastor. Prior to 1940, he held a pacifist position based upon the belief that Jesus' ethic of nonviolence was the same for the individual and the public official. Yet he also believed government was to be obeyed and that it would be wrong for a Christian to withhold his taxes even from a government that persecuted the church.

> The Christian is neither obliged nor able to examine the rightfulness of the demands of government in each particular case. His duty of obedience is binding upon him until government directly compels him to offend against the divine commandment, that is to say, until government openly denies its divine commission and thereby forfeits its claim. It is not, however, permissible to generalize from this offence and to conclude that this government now possesses no claim to obedience in some of its other demands . . . Disobedience can never be anything but a concrete decision in a single particular case.[9]

However, after 1940, Bonhoeffer became convinced that it was a Christian's right and duty to oppose tyranny and that national socialism was a system of government no longer based upon natural law or the law of God. He became involved in the July 1944 plot to assassinate Hitler, but the plot was discovered. He was imprisoned and hanged without trial on April 9, 1945, just a few days before the Allies arrived. Would you have agreed with Bonhoeffer?

There are so many other exceptions and "what ifs" that could be addressed here which are not within the scope of our consideration. We have simply (perhaps simplistically for some) stated biblical principles that help define a Christian's relationship to government.

I believe that armed with these principles and prayer, we will be equipped to come to an informed position. We will also be able to maintain our unity as a church; though we may come to different conclusions about

9. Bonhoeffer, *Ethics*, 343.

this issue, we have a bottom-line perspective that unites us. The winds of war will always blow across the world, but our Sovereign God is not confused. Let us commit ourselves to doing good, treating others with respect, praying for our leaders, praying for our enemies, and praying for peace so that the gospel will be preached to all the nations leading to our Lord's return.

D. IN THE DEBT OF LOVE (13:8–14)

Review

Paul has defined the four key relationships in the life of the self-surrendered servant who has been the recipient of the mercies of God. They are a relationship of submission to God, to others in the church, to those outside the church, and to governmental authorities. The latter is not an uncritical submission to any law being leveled by the state, but Paul's exhortation is a general mind-set of the Christian toward authority.[10]

Preview

Paul now continues to unpack the theme of love (*agape*), which he introduced in 12:9–13. While it seems at first glance that Paul is speaking primarily about relationships among believers, those outside the church cannot be excluded. Paul is not interpreting love for the neighbor as narrowly as did some Jews in his day. They defined "neighbor" (*plesion*) as a fellow Israelite and therefore as an implicit justification of hatred for all non-Jews. The defining concept in this section is *opheilete* (*owe*) and this connects the debt of love that we owe our neighbor with the debts (*opheilas*) owed to the ruling authorities in verse 7.

Paul's emphasis on the obligation of love parallels John's thought in 1 John 4:11: "Beloved, if God so loved us, we also ought [*opheilo*] to love one another." In Romans 13:8–14, Paul gives two overarching reasons why Christian love is not optional, but obligatory. The first reason is that love is the fulfillment of the law of God (vv. 8–10). The second reason is that the second coming of Christ is near (vv. 11–14).

---

10. Schreiner, *Romans*, 687.

1. Love is the Fulfillment of the Law (vv. 8–10).

> Owe no one anything, except to love each other, for the one who loves another has fulfilled the law. For the commandments, "You shall not commit adultery, You shall not murder, You shall not steal, You shall not covet," and any other commandment, are summed up in this word: "You shall love your neighbor as yourself." Love does no wrong to a neighbor; therefore love is the fulfilling of the law.

A Peanuts cartoon shows Schroeder practicing on his pint-sized piano while Lucy looks on him admiringly. She finally interrupts him and says, "Schroeder, do you know what love is?" The miniature musician stops, stares off into space and says, "Love: Noun, fondness, a strong affection for, or devotion or attachment to a person or persons." He then resumes playing while Lucy sighs and says to herself, "On paper, he's great."

The kind of love to which Paul calls the church is far more than theoretical; it is the fulfillment and summary of God's law. "Owe no one anything, except to love each other, for the one who loves another has fulfilled the law." Paul is not giving us a lesson on economics (although being debt-free is a wise idea), but underscoring the obligatory nature of love. While we may wish we could say to our mortgage company that we no longer want to pay our monthly installments (and some have gone in foreclosure), we can never say to another person, "I've quite had my fill of you and my love has come to an end." Even though we may feel like that, we must not foreclose on the debt of love.

Paul continues by "fleshing out" the command to love. The concept of love is often vague and relegated to the subjective world of feelings. However, by saying that love fulfills the law, Paul is adding a directional reality. This is what paying the debt of love looks like: sexual purity and faithfulness; doing everything in our power to benefit and preserve the life of others; refusing to take from anyone what is not ours and being generous to help those in need; always speaking truth; and being satisfied with what we have so as not to desire what others possess. This obligation to love others is summed up, fleshed out, and fulfilled in the second table of the law.

Think about the ramifications of what has just been said. Can you imagine the positive impact on culture, the church, and our families, if we truly grasped that love is a choice which is not separated from law (doing the right thing)? This understanding could impact our finances, sexuality, and the way we view our material possessions.

The apostle John hammers home the serious obligation of Christian love. "If anyone says, 'I love God,' and hates his brother, he is a liar; for he who does not love his brother whom he has seen cannot love God whom he has not seen. And this commandment we have from him: whoever loves God must also love his brother" (1 John 4:20–21).

2. The Second Coming of Christ is Near (11–14).

> Besides this you know the time; that the hour has come for you to wake from sleep. For salvation is nearer to us now than when we first believed. The night is far gone; the day is at hand. So then let us cast off the works of darkness and put on the armor of light. Let us walk properly as in the daytime, not in orgies and drunkenness, not in sexual immorality and sensuality, not in quarreling and jealousy. But put on the Lord Jesus Christ, and make no provision for the flesh, to gratify its desires.

The second reason why we are to love one another is because we live in the light of the imminent return of our Lord Jesus. Often in the New Testament whenever the return of Christ is mentioned it is in the context of a call to holy living (2 Pet 3:11–13). Since love is the key ingredient in the life of obedience to the law of God, the recognition of Christ's return should sharpen our focus on its practice. Paul uses four action phrases to challenge us in view of the Lord's return; one phrase in each verse: *Wake up! Cast off! Walk properly! Put on!* How do you understand them? Frederick Godet summarizes this section nicely:

> To lay aside what belongs to the night of earthly life, is only the first part of the preparation to which we are called by the rising of the great day. Our concern must be, besides, to put on the dispositions which are in keeping with so holy and brilliant a light. What is this new equipment which we must haste to substitute for the old? Paul indicates it in the expression: *put on the Lord Jesus Christ.* The toilet [place of changing and cleaning up] of the believer, if one might so venture to speak, in view of the approaching salvation, consists solely in putting on Christ, in appropriating by habitual communion with Him all His sentiments and all His manner of acting. He thus becomes for His redeemed ones Himself the robe for the marriage-feast. The Christian will be unable to stand before Him except in so far as he is "found in Him" (Philippians 3.9).[11]

---

11. Godet, *Epistle to the Romans*, 451.

E. IN THE FELLOWSHIP OF BELIEVERS FROM DIVERSE CULTURES (14:1—15:13)

Review

Paul's overall theme since the beginning of chapter 12 was self-surrender in view of God's great mercies to us in Christ. Further, Paul unpacked that self-surrender by emphasizing the debt of love we owe to our neighbor as well as the laying aside of sexual impurity, quarrelling, and division in view of the imminence of the Lord's return.

Preview

Paul now turns his attention to the quarreling and division taking place between two culturally diverse groups in the church at Rome. These groups were arguing over issues not central to the Christian faith (we might call them scruples), and yet very important to their cultural identity. Paul gives important principles for handling such differences and these principles can be helpful to today's church as well. He concludes that the overarching purpose for unity is the glory of God.

"As for the one who is weak in faith, welcome him, but not to quarrel over opinions." The Greek word for *opinion* is *dialogismos*—inward reasoning, disputable matters, scruples. In Latin *scrupulus* literally is a small sharp pebble in the shoe that causes irritation.

What are some of the scruples that Christians have today—convictions which can be divisive, but are not central to the Christian faith? Issues such as the use of alcohol or tobacco; movie- or theatre-going; music, even worship music; jewelry or outward adornment; worship on Saturday, vegetarianism; head coverings for women in church; birth control; environmentalism; speaking in tongues; views on baptism and the Lord's Supper; views on the second coming of Christ; buttons or hooks on clothing; modern conveniences (cars, electricity); a certain version of the Bible as the only authorized one; the place of political involvement; allowing the celebration of Halloween; the observance of Christmas and Easter. Around such things entire denominations have been built, dissensions have raged, and even wars have been fought (maybe not over Halloween).

The church at Rome was a multicultural church made up of Christians who were not only Jewish or gentile, but also from ethnically diverse backgrounds. Thus, these scruples were deep-seated because they also had a cultural connection as well as a religious one. The Jews had been raised with the tradition that eating certain kinds of meat was wrong (Lev 11 and Deut 14). Therefore, even after these Jews became Christ-followers, many continued to give conscientious commitment to the dietary restrictions mandated by the Old Testament law. Many of them also continued to observe certain feasts, fasts, and festivals.

The gentiles, on the other hand, had been brought up in a pagan environment where most of the meat in town was sold in temple markets and had first been offered to pagan gods. Many of these young gentile believers became vegetarians so they would not compromise their consciences by eating meat and (in their minds) participate in idolatry. However, there were also more mature gentile believers who were convinced that other gods did not exist and that Jesus Christ had given them liberty to eat anything, as long as they did so with thanksgiving. So there may have been tension even between the gentile believers. (You can read more about this controversy in 1 Corinthians 8–10.)

The real tension, however, was felt between the mature gentile believers and the majority of the Jewish Christians in the church. I do not adopt James Dunn's interpretation that the issue was one of the Jews setting boundaries and establishing their identity as God's unique covenant people. I believe that Paul was treating this as a nonessential issue and was establishing the priority of honoring one another and preserving unity on the essentials.[12] Can you imagine the problem this caused within the church? These culturally different groups could not even eat with each other!

Perhaps they were even calling each other names: *liberal/worldly/ lawbreakers* on one side and *fundies/far-right/legalists* on the other. Paul did not use names, but did use the categories of *strong* and *weak* to describe these differently-opinioned groups. The strong were strong in faith, whose consciences allowed them to eat without doubting. The weak were not ninety-eight-pound weaklings, but those whose faith would not allow them in good conscience to eat certain kinds of food. He tackled this issue in our text and gave us principles that would answer the question: How do Christians of differing convictions get along with each other and preserve unity in the church?

12. Stott, *Romans*, 358.

> As for the one who is weak in faith, welcome him, but not to quar-
> rel over opinions. One person believes he may eat anything, while
> the weak person eats only vegetables. Let not the one who eats de-
> spise the one who abstains, and let not the one who abstains pass
> judgment on the one who eats, for God has welcomed him. Who
> are you to pass judgment on the servant of another? It is before his
> own master that he stands or falls. And he will be upheld, for the
> Lord is able to make him stand. (14:1–4)

Do not make the error of passing judgment on those who disagree
with you. This was the danger of those who had convictions in this area
becoming critical and judgmental of those who had liberty. Instead, the
weak-faith ones (those without liberty) should accept the strong in faith
(those who have freedom to eat meat) because they have been accepted by
God as his children and stand before him as servants of God. Why would
you alienate those for whom Jesus died and forgave, removing their guilt
and shame? Again, "weak in faith" does not describe those who are not
getting enough animal protein, but the ones whose consciences will not
allow them to eat meat. No one should ever treat a brother or sister as a
second-class citizen just because they disagree over opinions.

> One person esteems one day as better than another, while another
> esteems all days alike. Each one should be fully convinced in his
> own mind. The one who observes the day, observes it in honor
> of the Lord. The one who eats, eats in honor of the Lord, since
> he gives thanks to God, while the one who abstains, abstains in
> honor of the Lord and gives thanks to God. For none of us lives to
> himself, and none of us dies to himself. For if we live, we live to the
> Lord, and if we die, we die to the Lord. So then, whether we live or
> whether we die, we are the Lord's. (14:5–8)

Paul gives us an excellent test of our scruples: If you hold a certain
tradition or scruple, why do you hold it? Is it to make yourself look better
or more spiritual in the eyes of others, or because you believe that such a
conviction honors the Lord? Also, if you have freedom to do something is
it because you want to please yourself at the expense of others or so that
you may please the Lord? As we will see, "freedom to do" is also a "freedom
not to do." You are not your own; neither should your scruples nor your
freedom be about you, but about the Lord whose servant you are.

> For to this end Christ died and lived again, that he might be Lord
> both of the dead and of the living. Why do you pass judgment on

your brother? Or you, why do you despise your brother? For we
will all stand before the judgment seat of God; for it is written,
"As I live," says the Lord, "every knee shall bow to me, and every
tongue shall confess to God." So then each of us will give an account of himself to God. (14:9–12)

It reminds us of the words of Jesus in Matthew 7:1: "Judge not, that
you be not judged." However, the context of this verse indicates that this
judging does not mean setting aside the ability to be discerning. Rather,
Jesus (and Paul) used the word in the sense of a condemning judgment that
leads to hypocrisy and derision. You are not to condemn your brother or
sister who may be different than you—from another culture, who speaks a
different language, who worships differently than you do. Such judgment
leads to pushing them to the periphery, then treating them with derision.
We will be held accountable by God for such judgmental attitudes towards
our brothers/sisters.

> Therefore let us not pass judgment on one another any longer, but
> rather decide never to put a stumbling block or hindrance in the
> way of a brother. I know and am persuaded in the Lord Jesus that
> nothing is unclean in itself, but it is unclean for anyone who thinks
> it unclean. For if your brother is grieved by what you eat, you are
> no longer walking in love. By what you eat, do not destroy the
> one for whom Christ died. So do not let what you regard as good
> be spoken of as evil. For the kingdom of God is not a matter of
> eating and drinking but of righteousness and peace and joy in the
> Holy Spirit. Whoever thus serves Christ is acceptable to God and
> approved by men. So then let us pursue what makes for peace and
> for mutual upbuilding. (14:13–19)

This passage can be best summed up by two sentences and an illustration. We should be less concerned with judging others and more concerned
with judging ourselves, whether we are helping or hurting others. We
should also recognize that there are more important things in the Christian
life than having our own way.

And now the illustration, using a hypothetical situation not from
Paul's day, but from our own: Let's say I am out with a group of Christians
and feel like having a glass of wine with my meal, and yet I recognize there
is a brother in the group who is in recovery and I might add to his struggle
by ordering a drink. What do I do? Additionally, what if a brother or sister
is present in the group who I know has a conviction against drinking; what
do I do? I could say to myself, "I know that drinking is not outlawed in

scripture (drunkenness is), and I know that I always limit myself to one drink. I know also this is a matter of Christian liberty, and these people need to grow up. Besides, I want a glass of wine. It is their problem, not mine." Or I could say to myself, "I know I am free to have a glass of wine, but I also know that Fred struggles with the stuff and Ella has a conviction against alcohol. Perhaps by ordering a drink, I might be a stumbling block to these people in some way. My actions could lead one back into sin and lead the other to sin against her own conscience. Therefore, since I have freedom in this matter, I'll order a Diet Pepsi because their spiritual well-being is more important than me having my own way. It is not their problem, but mine." Which response sounds more in keeping with Paul's thought?

I want to add one more thought. If I am with a group where I don't know everyone, I will not order alcohol simply because I do not want to cause anyone to stumble. There are three guiding principles I use to check myself before I participate in an activity:

- Does the Bible forbid it?

- Would it lead me to temptation and to sin?

- Could it be used to cause someone else to stumble in their faith?

> Do not, for the sake of food, destroy the work of God. Everything is indeed clean, but it is wrong for anyone to make another stumble by what he eats. It is good not to eat meat or drink wine or do anything that causes your brother to stumble. The faith that you have, keep between yourself and God. Blessed is the one who has no reason to pass judgment on himself for what he approves. But whoever has doubts is condemned if he eats, because the eating is not from faith. For whatever does not proceed from faith is sin. (14:20–23)

This is an excellent summary statement for both the strong and the weak when it comes to scruples and Christian freedom: Strong folks—if you have freedom of conscience in a certain area, keep it to yourself; don't flaunt it lest you hinder the work of God in your brother's life. Weak folks—if you have doubts about doing something, don't do it just because you see a mature Christian doing it. "For whatever does not proceed from faith is sin."

I remember counseling a woman who grew up as a vegetarian, and when she became a Christian she remained a vegan and in good conscience would not eat meat. The people who were helping her grow spiritually tried to impart to her the principle of freedom in Christ. They told her that she should exercise that freedom because the Bible does not forbid us from eating animal products. She was conflicted about this, so she came to me and asked what I thought. I told her that on the basis of Romans 14:23 I didn't think she should go against her conscience regardless of where the conviction originated. Instead, I counseled her to make it a matter of prayer and to read the Scripture so that her conscience could be more informed by the word of God than by someone else's opinion.

I also gave her a text in Acts 10 about Peter who also had a scruple against eating meat, and how God informed his conscience so that he could actually go into a non-kosher house of Cornelius and preach the gospel over a meal. A few weeks later, she came back and told me that she no longer doubted that she could eat meat, but would remain a vegetarian because she didn't like the way meat tasted. However, for the sake of the gospel, she would be willing to eat anything.

> We who are strong have an obligation to bear with the failings of the weak, and not to please ourselves. Let each of us please his neighbor for his good, to build him up. For Christ did not please himself, but as it is written, "The reproaches of those who reproached you fell on me." For whatever was written in former days was written for our instruction, that through endurance and through the encouragement of the Scriptures we might have hope. May the God of endurance and encouragement grant you to live in such harmony with one another, in accord with Christ Jesus, that together you may with one voice glorify the God and Father of our Lord Jesus Christ. (15:1–6)

Here we see that Paul identified with the strong-in-faith folks, which we knew all along because of his discourse in 1 Corinthians 10:23–33: "Give no offense to Jews or Greeks or to the church of God, just as I try to please everyone in everything I do, not seeking my own advantage, but that of many, that they may be saved." Thus those with Christian liberty should not please themselves, but should bear with (*bastazo*—"tolerate," "endure," "support") those who do not have freedom of conscience.

Paul was not advocating being a fawning people-pleaser who tries to win the approval of others. Instead he appealed to the strong ones that they should use their freedom to build up and edify those who are weak. "This upbuilding of the weak will doubtless include helping to educate and so to strengthen their conscience."[13] We are to follow the example of our Lord

13. Stott, *Romans*, 369.

Jesus, who though a man of deep conviction and maturity, gave himself away for others showing his nature as a servant. One almost expects Paul to break out in the same hymn of praise as he did in Philippians 2:6–11. Instead Paul applies the words of Psalm 69:9 to describe Christ as the righteous man who suffered for the sin of others.

One is not sure why Paul broke into benediction here. Certainly he was not finished with his thought. Perhaps Paul recognized that though believers should strive for unity and harmony, they are ultimately gifts from God.[14] He made a similar point in Ephesians 4:3 where he urged the church to be "eager to maintain the unity of the Spirit in the bond of peace." Our responsibility is to maintain the unity that God has given to us. However, this unity is not for the purpose of making life easier for all, but so that God is glorified.

> To glorify God is to exhibit his praise and honour. In the background lurks the thought of the prejudice incurred for the final end . . . when the fellowship of the saints is marred by suspicions and dissensions and in this case particularly by the arrogance of the strong and the stumblings of the weak. No considerations could enforce the exhortation more strongly than to be reminded of the glory of God as the controlling purpose of all our attitudes and actions.[15]
>
> Therefore welcome one another as Christ has welcomed you, for the glory of God. For I tell you that Christ became a servant to the circumcised to show God's truthfulness, in order to confirm the promises given to the patriarchs, and in order that the Gentiles might glorify God for his mercy. As it is written, "Therefore I will praise you among the Gentiles, and sing to your name." And again it is said, "Rejoice, O Gentiles, with his people." And again, "Praise the Lord, all you Gentiles, and let all the peoples extol him." And again Isaiah says, "The root of Jesse will come, even he who arises to rule the Gentiles; in him will the Gentiles hope." May the God of hope fill you with all joy and peace in believing, so that by the power of the Holy Spirit you may abound in hope. (15:7–13)

Once again we see that Paul emphasized the glory of God. It is the terminal point of our love and service to one another within the church, and the overarching purpose of the unity of the church in an ethnically divided world not unlike our own. Paul concluded this thought with another

14. Schreiner, *Romans*, 749.
15. Murray, *Romans*, 201.

benediction stressing that the only real hope for such unity is realized in the God of hope. All of our striving, as well as our failure, find their hope in him.

It is in this context I bring up something that could easily be misunderstood or might give offense, but hear me out. I wonder how much of what Paul says could be applied to the majority culture's attitude toward the minority culture (in the church) and vice versa? I will leave it for you to unpack this further, but does an ethnic majority have an obligation to understand and honor the differences of the minority as an act of welcoming/receiving them as Christ did those in the majority?

Let me give you an example of which I am not very proud. In one of my churches, many years ago, there was a young African man who started coming to our Sunday evening service while he was a student at the university. Each night he wanted to sing a solo and would just hand the hymnbook to our pianist and expect her to accompany him. At first, I thought it was a unique cultural characteristic, but when he pressed to do it regularly, I started to get negative feedback from my congregation. I no longer let him sing every week and tried to put him into a special music rotation, which he resisted. I began to look upon this man with resentment. So, we had a long conversation one day that did not go well, and looking back, I take responsibility for that. I was in the majority and had all the power, but did not use it to understand him, to receive him, or to honor him. Knowing that hindsight is usually twenty-twenty, I think we could have worked something out. Instead, I used my position to limit his participation to the point where he was offended and left with tremendous resentment toward me and the church that was evident for years to come. I confessed my sinful attitude toward him, but our relationship was beyond repair.

Nonessentials should never be moved to the level of the essentials, nor should they ever hinder us demonstrating love to one another. "In essential things unity, in doubtful things liberty, in all things charity."[16] All for God's glory!

---

16. Attributed to Saint Augustine but it cannot be found in any of his writings. Some believe it originated with Peter Meiderlin (Rupertus Meldeniu), 1626. Still others claim to have traced the quote to Marco Antonio de Dominus (d. 1624), who was a twice-lapsed heretic. You decide. . . .

II

Paul's Future Plans and Final Greetings (15:14—16:27)

A. PAUL'S HEART AND CALLING (15:14-22)

Review

PAUL EMPHASIZED THE GLORY of God as being the overarching purpose of the unity of Jew and gentile in the world. Nonessentials should never be moved to the level of the essentials, nor should they ever hinder us in sharing the gospel for God's glory.

Preview

Paul finishes the instructional part of his letter to the church at Rome. He now prepares for his visit to Rome by sharing with the believers there his heart, his desire, his ambition, and his strategy for ministry; that those who have never been told the gospel will hear, and those who have never heard will understand.

Have you seen some of these letters written to pastors by children? They are hilarious.

- Dear Pastor, I would like to go to heaven someday because I know my brother won't be there. —Stephen (age 8, Chicago).

- Dear Pastor, I know God loves everybody but he never met my sister. Yours sincerely, Arnold (age 8, Nashville).

- Dear Pastor, Please say in your sermon that Peter Peterson has been a good boy all week. Sincerely, Peter Peterson (age 9, Phoenix).

- Dear Pastor, I'm sorry I can't leave more money in the plate, but my father didn't give me a raise in my allowance. Could you have a sermon about raising your kid's allowance? Love, Patty (age 10, New Haven).

- Dear Pastor, Please say a prayer for our Little League team. We either need God's help or a new pitcher. Thank you, Alexander (age 10, Raleigh).

- Dear Pastor, Are there any devils on earth? I think there may be one in my Sunday School class. —Carla (age 10, Salina).

- Dear Pastor, I liked your sermon on Sunday; especially when it was finished. —Ralph (age 11, Akron).

The text before us (15:14–22) is not a letter to a pastor, but a portion of a letter written by Paul to the church at Rome. Though he was not their pastor, his words demonstrated his pastoral heart and calling.

> I myself am satisfied about you, my brothers, that you yourselves are full of goodness, filled with all knowledge and able to instruct one another. But on some points I have written to you very boldly by way of reminder, because of the grace given me by God to be a minister of Christ Jesus to the Gentiles in the priestly service of the gospel of God, so that the offering of the Gentiles may be acceptable, sanctified by the Holy Spirit. In Christ Jesus, then, I have reason to be proud of my work for God. For I will not venture to speak of anything except what Christ has accomplished through me to bring the Gentiles to obedience—by word and deed, by the power of signs and wonders, by the power of the Spirit of God—so that from Jerusalem and all the way around to Illyricum I have fulfilled the ministry of the gospel of Christ; and thus I make it my ambition to preach the gospel, not where Christ has already been named, lest I build on someone else's foundation, but as it

is written, "Those who have never been told of him will see, and those who have never heard will understand."

Paul reveals much of himself to the church at Rome in this passage:

- Paul's Heart (v. 14): "I myself am satisfied about you, my brothers, that you yourselves are full of goodness, filled with all knowledge and able to instruct one another."

  The church at Rome was filled with problems because it was filled with people, and wherever you have people, you have problems. How, then, could he say such positive things about this church? Was he just trying to be nice? No, I think he said it because, though aware of their weaknesses, he loved them and had enormous confidence in God's grace at work in their midst. He told the Philippian church, "And I am sure of this, that he who began a good work in you will bring it to completion at the day of Jesus Christ" (Phil 1:6); and to the Colossians, "Giving thanks to the Father, who has qualified you to share in the inheritance of the saints in light" (Col 1:12). Paul was confident that God was at work in the church at Rome.

  It is especially easy for pastors to criticize and find fault with those in their congregations. We pastors often see you at your worst and if that is all we focused on it could be scary. It would be like focusing on someone's nose instead of keeping it within the context of their face. But there is a deeper eye that God has given pastors—a perspective that overrides the human view. It is an ability to see what you are becoming because of God's amazing work of grace in your lives. The pastor who loves his people sees the best in them and is not angry at their failures, but sad when they do not live up to their full potential. In return, a pastor's congregation will love him/her and see beyond weaknesses to what he/she can become.

- Paul's Desire (vv. 15–16): "But on some points I have written to you very boldly by way of reminder, because of the grace given me by God to be a minister of Christ Jesus to the Gentiles in the priestly service of the gospel of God, so that the offering of the Gentiles may be acceptable, sanctified by the Holy Spirit."

  In this long sentence, Paul told the church that he had written hard things in his letter as a way of reminding them of the gospel, so that their hearts may be established in grace. The pastor is to "preach the word; be ready in season and out of season; reprove, rebuke, and exhort, with complete patience and teaching" (2 Tim 4:2). We do this in order to remind our people of things they already know so that they might be fully established in them. I'm often curious about the phrase that some people use to criticize preaching—"it is not deep enough." They want "meat and not milk." If you examine how this last phrase is used in Hebrews 5, 1 Peter 2, and 1 Corinthians 3, you will see it describes teaching that is to be geared to the spiritual maturity of the learner. Some Christians need strong boundary-teaching (stay away from those things, don't get drunk, don't sue another Christian) = milk; others need to be taught principles to live by (your body is the temple of the Holy Spirit, whether you eat or drink do it all for the glory of God, personal issues between Christians should be handled in the church and not in the courts for the sake of the gospel) = meat. A preacher/teacher's task is not to fill your minds with facts and knowledge, but to fill your hearts with reminders of God's grace and truth so that you will grow up into Christ, whether you are a baby in Christ or a more mature believer.

I knew a man (not in my church) who was a brilliant theologian, who constantly corrected his pastor on points of doctrine, critically challenging him to preach sermons that were deeper and more profound. One day this pastor wisely challenged this older scholar by pointing out that the end of knowledge is to produce in us the character and maturity of Jesus Christ, "which, my dear brother, I do not see in you." This reminds me of the words attributed to Jonathan Edwards's grandfather, Solomon Stoddard: "We are not sent into the pulpit to show wit and eloquence, but to set the consciences of men on fire!"

Fixing a meal takes so much time and yet is quickly eaten. Housework is a never-ending task and yet it needs to be done continually. And so the work of reminding people of God's truth is to be done in season and out; it is a never-ending task. When a pastor finishes at one church, he moves to the next and does the same thing. Although we look for fresh ways of saying the same things and try to use clever and engaging illustrations, the faithful pastor's main task is to remind his people of the gospel which nourishes, saves, and sanctifies. He desires that his church not be filled with theologically astute people, but with transformed people who are living out what they already know.

Even more than transformation, Paul desired that those to whom he ministered become a "priestly offering to God" (v. 16). This is a phrase that most of us don't associate with the work of a pastor. Just as the priest brought animals to sacrifice before the Lord, even so the pastor labors to bring his people as an offering to the Lord; not as dead sacrifices, but living sacrifices. "I appeal to you therefore, brothers, by the mercies of God, to present your bodies as a living sacrifice, holy and acceptable to God, which is your spiritual worship" (Rom 12:1, NIV).

- Paul's Ambition (vv. 17–18): "In Christ Jesus, then, I have reason to be proud of my work for God. For I will not venture to speak of anything except what Christ has accomplished through me to bring the Gentiles to obedience—by word and deed."

Think about that—"what Christ has accomplished through me." Eugene Peterson paraphrases it this way: "I have no interest in giving you a chatty account of my adventures, only the wondrously powerful and transformingly present words and deeds of Christ in me that triggered a believing response among the outsiders" (Rom 15:17–18, The Message).

A lot of pastors are good at giving chatty accounts of their adventures, and how hard they work, and how little credit they receive. However, the pastor's chief ambition is to speak about Jesus; about what he has done, and what he can do. Everything you see that is good in any church or in any pastor's life is the result of what God has done through Jesus Christ. And whatever exists simply because we humans have done it has no ultimate value. That is why those who do not know Jesus Christ are not only separated from eternal life, but are left to live with the reality that they have no lasting significance apart from him.

- Paul's Strategy (vv. 19–20) " so that from Jerusalem and all the way around to Illyricum I have fulfilled the ministry of the gospel of Christ; and thus I make it my ambition to preach the gospel, not where Christ has already been named, lest I build on someone else's foundation."

His strategy was rather "Star Trekian"; to go where no man had gone before and to preach Christ where he had never been preached. Paul preached in Asia Minor, then in Greece, all the way to the border of modern-day Albania; and finally he went to Rome. He preached Jesus in the major seaport cities, and in the great capital cities and cultural centers of that day. He preached Christ to people of influence so that they could reach others (such as the philosophers and influential women at Athens, the proconsul Sergius Paulus at Paphos, the honorable women of Berea, those in the school of Tyrannus at Ephesus, and others of like significance). He established churches in such cities so they would become centers for carrying the gospel throughout the world. Once a church was planted, he moved on. This was his strategy.

It is the same with Christians today who have a strategy for reaching Muslims, Hindus, Buddhists, animists, and those who have no religion at all with the gospel of Jesus. There are still 6700 people groups composing 42 percent of the world's population who have not yet heard the message of Jesus. There are some Christians who are committed to Bible translation in distant lands, and we may know some who are pioneer missionaries who are taking the gospel into "closed countries." Many are committed to support Christian radio and TV like SAT/7, which beams the gospel into Islamic countries closed to traditional missions.

Many Christians are involved in international aid and development or have moved into the city or some housing development of people with high needs and low understanding of the gospel to show them the love of Jesus. There are some Christians who are planting churches in highly unchurched regions of our country. I have even known Christians who developed a strategy to pick up hitchhikers of a certain nationality and befriend them in order to tell them about Jesus. There are also those who strategically pray for their neighborhoods so that their neighbors will come to Jesus.

In summary, ponder the following questions. They may help to direct or redirect your life for the sake of the gospel for the very brief time you have left on this earth:

Heart: Do you have a heart for God's people? Do you love the church with all its warts and imperfections, or are you constantly sitting on the judgment seat?

Desire: Is it your desire to remind others of the truth of the gospel? Those of you who are teachers, are you more concerned with how you wow people with your biblical knowledge or with how you can challenge them toward maturity?

Ambition: Is it your ambition to speak only of Christ and what he has done through you, and not of your personal successes and position?

Strategy: Do you have a strategy for your life and ministry? How are you going to take what you have to offer and position yourself to be of greatest impact for the gospel? Your strategy might change during the different chapters of your life, but you still need one overarching goal to bring intentionality into your life or else you'll get swallowed up with life itself. Granted, we are not a Paul or a Billy Graham; not all missionaries to closed countries, or Bible translators, or workers in international development or Christian radio; nor are we all pastors. However, that does not mean we have been given a pass from having a strategy for our lives.

Our passage ends with a quotation from Isaiah 52:15, which I think sums up what our strategy should be as individuals and as a church. We exist so that "Those who have never been told of him will see, and those who have never heard will understand" (NIV).

B. PAUL'S PLAN TO VISIT ROME ON HIS WAY TO SPAIN (15:22–33)

Review

Paul expressed love for and confidence in the church at Rome and explained his forthrightness to them on the grounds of his calling as a minister of the Lord Jesus and an apostle to the gentiles. He also explained why he had never visited them before by sharing his heart, desire, ambition, and strategy for ministry.

Preview

Paul is now ready to finally go to Rome after so many years of waiting but being hindered from doing so. However, first Paul has to bring a love offering collected from the gentile churches for the Mother Church in Jerusalem which was experiencing hardship. He then will visit Rome on his way to Spain. He asks the church at Rome to pray that God would bring his plans to completion. God did, but in a way very different from what Paul expected.

> This is the reason why I have so often been hindered from coming to you. But now, since I no longer have any room for work in these regions, and since I have longed for many years to come to you, I hope to see you in passing as I go to Spain, and to be helped on my journey there by you, once I have enjoyed your company for a while. At present, however, I am going to Jerusalem bringing aid to

the saints. For Macedonia and Achaia have been pleased to make some contribution for the poor among the saints at Jerusalem. For they were pleased to do it, and indeed they owe it to them. For if the Gentiles have come to share in their spiritual blessings, they ought also to be of service to them in material blessings. When therefore I have completed this and have delivered to them what has been collected, I will leave for Spain by way of you. I know that when I come to you I will come in the fullness of the blessing of Christ.

Schreiner says that Paul makes use of a "divine passive" (*enekopto-men*) when he says that he had often been hindered in coming to visit the Romans.[1] In other words, God had hindered Paul because of other opportunities that were appointed for him to preach the gospel. Now, however, Paul was ready for the visit because he believed his work was done—not that everyone was evangelized, but that the gospel had been preached and churches established to carry on the work. This was Paul's missionary strategy delineated in 15:20—to preach the gospel where it had never before been preached.

In some respects, we could look at this section as part of a missionary fundraising appeal. He was going to travel about 1500 miles by ship from Jerusalem to Rome, and then 700 more miles to Spain. Rome was a strategic stop-off point where he could be refreshed and assisted (*propempo*) on the way. Stott claims that this word "had become a technical term for helping missionaries on their way . . . food, money, by arranging for companions, and means of travel."[2] This purpose was consistent with the fact that Paul's reason in visiting Rome was to be of mutual encouragement (1:12). Furthermore, Arthur Glasser suggests that Paul was here revealing his strategy that the church at Rome was to be "a second Antioch, the home base of operations for the mission of his apostolic band to Spain and the Western Mediterranean."[3]

The details of Paul's offering (*koinonia*) for the Jerusalem Church can be found in 1 Corinthians 16:1–4 and 2 Corinthians 8 and 9. Not only would this offering help the Christians in Jerusalem who were suffering the hardship of persecution, but it symbolized the gentile Christians' indebtedness to the Jewish church in Jerusalem. It was from Jerusalem that the gospel had spread to the regions beyond and this material offering was a

1. Schreiner, *Romans*, 774.
2. Stott, *Romans*, 385.
3. Glasser, "Paul and the Missionary Task," 153.

small return for that spiritual debt. In addition, it would go a long way in cementing relations with the more strict Jewish brethren who had always been suspicious of Paul's mission to the gentiles.

The significance of this offering was indicated by the fact that Paul would have to add about 800 miles from Corinth (where he was writing this letter) to Jerusalem onto the 1500 miles from Jerusalem to Rome. However, I believe that Paul saw this as the fulfillment of Old Testament prophecies concerning the gentiles bringing their wealth to Jerusalem and the inclusion of the gentiles into the people of God (Isa 60:5–7; 61:6).[4] It should also be noted that this was the second such offering Paul (and Barnabas) had brought to the Jerusalem Church. Eleven years earlier the offering had come from the Christians in Syrian Antioch when the Jerusalem Church was undergoing famine (Acts 11:30; 12:25) .

You would find it helpful to read Acts 21–28 and trace the very unusual pathway upon which God led Paul from Jerusalem to Rome. It is an example of God's sovereign will being accomplished by means far different than our own. In spite of the danger prophesied by Agabus and others (Acts 21:11–12), God kept Paul safe and directed his way quite providentially all the way to Rome—at Caesar's expense!

We have no historical record of Paul ever making the trip to Spain. In Acts 28:30 we read that Paul stayed for two years under house arrest in Rome where he received visitors and was able to freely preach and teach. What happened after the two years? We don't know, but there have been theories that have tried to piece together the historical puzzle.

There are some (including John Stott) who hold to a fourth missionary journey after Paul was released from confinement in Rome and before he was rearrested and killed in the Neronian persecutions. Others (including myself) believe that after these two years of relative freedom in Rome he was finally tried and convicted of some seditious crime, put into the dreaded Mamertine prison, and beheaded during the persecution of Christians in 64 AD. "The picture is ambiguous. On the one hand, it is hard to see how Paul could have been condemned to death on the evidence offered in Acts; on the other hand, Acts seems to be aware that he was going to appear before Caesar and die a martyr."[5]

What we do know is that he accomplished all that God intended, and if one holds to Philippians being written from Paul's imprisonment in

---

4. Schreiner, *Romans*, 776.

5. Marshall, *Acts*, 426.

Rome, one is treated to the utter joy and confidence that Paul exhibited in the sovereignty of God. "I want you to know, brothers, that what has happened to me has really served to advance the gospel, so that it has become known throughout the whole imperial guard and to all the rest that my imprisonment is for Christ" (Phil 1:12–13).

> I appeal to you, brothers, by our Lord Jesus Christ and by the love of the Spirit, to strive together with me in your prayers to God on my behalf, that I may be delivered from the unbelievers in Judea, and that my service for Jerusalem may be acceptable to the saints, so that by God's will I may come to you with joy and be refreshed in your company. May the God of peace be with you all. Amen.

Paul was not soliciting casual prayer from the Romans. He is appealing to them *to strive together* with him (*sunagonizomai*) or agonize together with him for the accomplishment of God's gracious plan concerning the difficult circumstances that he would face. Although he was willing to suffer and die for Jesus (Acts 21:13), he did not crave martyrdom. He wanted to live so that he might proclaim the gospel in the regions beyond. Have you ever agonized with anyone in prayer? It is a sign of deep fellowship and concern that we know little of in the church where prayer is often perfunctory and programmed.

However, Paul deeply desired that God's will would be accomplished and yielded himself submissively to God's sovereignty. We know how things turned out. Paul's foreboding about the future was not wrapped in the cloak of determinism, but dressed in the robe of trust; he was at peace. Paul knew not what the future held, but he knew who held the future.

C. TO THE ONLY WISE GOD BE GLORY (16:1-27)

Review

Paul related his plans for a visit to Rome after a stop-off in Jerusalem and before his trip to Spain. He asked for the church at Rome to pray for his protection and for his coming to them.

Preview

At first glance, the chapter seems to be just the closing of another letter where Paul greets a lot of people, and has about as much drama as reading a genealogical section in the Old Testament. However, this chapter has an eternal significance which we will someday experience if we know Jesus.

This chapter can be divided into three sections with a closing doxology:

1. The Diversity and Unity of the Church (16:1–16)

> I commend to you our sister Phoebe, a servant of the church at Cenchreae, that you may welcome her in the Lord in a way worthy of the saints, and help her in whatever she may need from you, for she has been a patron of many and of myself as well. Greet Prisca and Aquila, my fellow workers in Christ Jesus, who risked their necks for my life, to whom not only I give thanks but all the churches of the Gentiles give thanks as well. Greet also the church in their house. Greet my beloved Epaenetus, who was the first convert to Christ in Asia. Greet Mary, who has worked hard for you. Greet Andronicus and Junia, my kinsmen and my fellow prisoners. They are well known to the apostles, and they were in Christ before me. Greet Ampliatus, my beloved in the Lord. Greet Urbanus, our fellow worker in Christ, and my beloved Stachys. Greet Apelles, who is approved in Christ. Greet those who belong to the family of Aristobulus. Greet my kinsman Herodion. Greet those in the Lord who belong to the family of Narcissus. Greet those workers in the Lord, Tryphaena and Tryphosa. Greet the beloved Persis, who has worked hard in the Lord. Greet Rufus, chosen in the Lord; also his mother, who has been a mother to me as well. Greet Asyncritus, Phlegon, Hermes, Patrobas, Hermas, and the brothers who are with them. Greet Philologus, Julia, Nereus and his sister, and Olympas, and all the saints who are with them. Greet one another with a holy kiss. All the churches of Christ greet you.

Paul sent greetings to twenty-six people in a church to which he had never been. This has led some scholars to claim that the ending of Romans was meant for another church (Ephesus) and not for Rome, but there is no textual evidence for this view. Travel within the Roman Empire for a Roman citizen like Paul was much more common than we would expect.[6] Also, many of the people he greeted were known from his travels elsewhere. For someone who did not have Linked In or Facebook, he had a lot of friends.

---

6. Schreiner, *Romans*, 790.

However, it was not so much the number of people Paul knew that was impressive, but the variety of people he knew, showing the diversity of the first-century church—a diversity of race, social class, and gender. Some of them he called *syngenis* (relative, kinfolk). They were not relatives, but fellow Jews who were like a mother, sister, and brother to him. He had other friends who were gentiles. You can tell the non-Jews in this passage by their Greek and Latin names: Quartus, Phlegon, Philologus, and Epaenetus.

Some of his friends had common names that were ordinarily linked to slaves: Ampliatus, Urbanus, and Hermes. And very likely, the households of Aristobulus and Narcissus were filled with slaves, while the two aristocrats named were probably not believers.[7] Rufus, we believe, was an African and may have been the son of Simon of Cyrene who carried Jesus' cross.[8]

Nine out of twenty-six people mentioned were women; ten if you count Phoebe, who was most likely the bearer of Paul's letter. She was a deacon from the church at Cenchrea.[9] She was also identified as a *prostatis* of many; a helper, but also a wealthy patron or benefactor of many, including Paul. All of the women mentioned worked hard for the sake of the gospel, and worked alongside Paul as co-laborers. This seems to undercut the theory that Paul believed women had a lesser role in the church.

There were also two couples mentioned: Priscilla and Aquila. Notice that her name was mentioned first and in a familiar form, "Prisca" (like you would shorten someone's name you knew well; "Melchizedek" to "Mel"). Priscilla and Aquila were a couple with whom Paul had a special relationship from his time in Ephesus. There they probably risked their necks to protect him from a riot that you can read about in Acts 19. Also, Paul mentioned a young missionary couple by the name of Andronicus and Junias or Junia, who spent time in jail with Paul and came to be believers even before Paul.

These greetings demonstrated the love that existed in the early church and illustrated the fact that when one became a believer in Christ, one entered into relationship with all sorts of people. This relationship transcended the boundaries of race, rank, and gender. Paul said this very powerfully in Galatians 3:28: "There is neither Jew nor Greek, there is neither slave or free, there is no male and female, for you are all one in Jesus Christ."

This does not mean that distinctions are eliminated; that Christians become a race-less, class-less and sex-less group of people. However, it does

7. Schreiner, *Romans*, 793.
8. Mark 15:21 indicates that Simon had two sons, Alexander and Rufus.
9. This is the first time *ekklesia* (church) is mentioned in Romans.

mean that the usual walls which separate people in our world are broken down and should no longer be hindrances to full equality and unity in the body of Christ. Thus regardless of race, gender, or social position, we are brothers and sisters in Christ and equal sharers together in the grace of God. There should be no caste system in the church; those selected for leadership should be selected because of spiritual maturity and not their wealth or ethnicity, and their leadership should be carried out with humility and not self-importance.

2. A Warning against the Smoothies (16:17–20)

> I appeal to you, brothers, to watch out for those who cause divisions and create obstacles contrary to the doctrine that you have been taught; avoid them. For such persons do not serve our Lord Christ, but their own appetites, and by smooth talk and flattery they deceive the hearts of the naive. For your obedience is known to all, so that I rejoice over you, but I want you to be wise as to what is good and innocent as to what is evil. The God of peace will soon crush Satan under your feet. The grace of our Lord Jesus Christ be with you.

Paul warned against those in the church who stirred up strife and dissension; who were motivated by self-serving egos and not the desire to serve the greater cause of the gospel. He described these people as smooth in speech and winsome in their personalities, but their desire was to deceive the unsuspecting and to draw them into their cause.

Paul's threefold counsel is helpful for any church to preserve unity in the face of a great deal of diversity: First, he told them to *keep on the lookout* (*skopein*) for such people who were prone to cause dissension, just like he told the church at Philippi to keep on the lookout for the good examples of those who walked according to the truth (Phil 3:17).

Secondly, he told them to *avoid* people who foment dissension (1 Cor 5:11; 2 Thess 3:6, 14; 2 Tim 3:5; Titus 3:10). Don't hang with them and give them an opportunity to infect your attitudes (don't even give them the holy kiss of fellowship). There are plenty of things to criticize in any church—plenty of warts to point out. However, real brothers and sisters in the Lord do not pick at warts; they do not major in Criticism 101. Instead, they desire to pray for and encourage those who struggle so there may be growth and development. Paul might have been thinking about the situation in Romans 14 and how some people were taking nonessential issues and making them a stumbling block to others. Watch out for this and stay away from such people because they seek to bring division into the church.

Finally, he told them to *be wise* and to discern what is good and innocent in contrast to what is evil. The NEB reads, "I should wish you to be experts in goodness, but simpletons in evil."[10] What great counsel for any church because of the spiritual battles that rage all around! Some people do not believe that we are in a spiritual war, but all they need to do is to look at some of the things with which they struggle. Look at your marriage; look at your greed, lust, resentment, racial and gender bias; look at the way you hold grudges or want people and organizations to do things your way; the way you so easily get distracted from serving God and others. If you think this is the normal Christian life, you are sadly mistaken. Satan is alive, but not well. He has been mortally wounded by the death and resurrection of Christ, but he is dangerous. That is why you must continue to be vigilant, to stay away from those who could deceive you, and to become an expert in the good and innocent in evil. And you need to keep it up, for the promise is that God will ultimately throw Satan under the church bus and he will be defeated at Christ's return.

3. Oh, by the Way . . . (16:21–23 [24])

> Timothy, my fellow worker, greets you; so do Lucius and Jason and Sosipater, my kinsmen. I Tertius, who wrote this letter, greet you in the Lord. Gaius, who is host to me and to the whole church, greets you. Erastus, the city treasurer, and our brother Quartus, greet you. [Some manuscripts insert verse 24: "The grace of our Lord Jesus Christ be with you all. Amen."]

This is really an amazing section that can easily go unnoticed. Paul mentioned eight more people who sent their greetings from Corinth to the church at Rome: Timothy, who was Paul's key disciple, born of an unbelieving Greek father and Jewish Christian mother. He was not raised as a Jew because Paul actually had him circumcised as an adult (Acts 16). Lucius, Jason, andSosipater who were all Jews. Gaius was the man with whom Paul was staying (he may be identified with Titius Justus of Acts 18:7) and Erastus was a city official. These five men may have been the leaders of separate house churches in Corinth, demonstrating the interrelationship different congregations in different cities had with one another. Then there was Tertius, who signed his own greeting as Paul's scribe and who actually wrote the letter as Paul dictated it. Finally, there was Quartus.

---

10 The New English Bible, 346.

I am told that the Chinese used to rename their servants according to their usefulness. "The number one boy" was usually the one put in charge of a household and actually hired the other servants, handled the finances, etc. Then the number two boy, three boy, and four boy had duties assigned to them according to their rank. Obviously, the goal was that everyone would move up a notch. The same was true of slaves in the Roman world: there was the slave named Primus (number one), who was the head of all the slaves. Next there was Secundus (number two), then Tertius (number three), then Quartus (number four). Apparently Tertius became a Christian; he may have belonged to Gaius's house church, he knew how to read and write, he became close to Paul, and was actually the writer of the letter that Paul dictated. I can just see it now. Paul said, "Timothy, my fellow worker greets you; so do Lucias and Jason and Sosipater." And then Tertius spontaneously wrote, "And I, (the number-three boy) who wrote this letter, greets you in the Lord."

Then Paul picks it up again and says, "Gaius, who is my host and hosts the church in his home also greets you and also Erastus the city treasurer greets you." This may be the same Erastus whose official name and rank was found on a stone during an archeological dig in Corinth: a very influential person who was also a believer. And then in the same sentence Paul says, "and our brother Quartus [the number-four boy] who is our brother, greets you." Donald Grey Barnhouse called this the "church in a paragraph."[11]

So in this closing section of this amazing letter to the Romans, we have greetings from an influential pastor named Timothy, a wealthy householder and church leader, Gaius, an influential city official, Erastus, and a number-three and a number-four slave. And the letter itself was carried to Rome by a woman, Phoebe. This is *koinonia*—the fellowship of the church; a new society or brotherhood of diverse people held together by love of a common Lord, Jesus Christ, and a commitment of love to one another. Our culture honors diversity, but it does so in a way that polarizes and fuels animosity. Such is sinful humanity's response to diversity. Only the gospel can honor diversity and produce unity in Jesus Christ because only the gospel can change the heart.

4. Paul's Benediction and Doxology (16:25–27)

> Now to him who is able to strengthen you according to my gospel and the preaching of Jesus Christ, according to the revelation of the mystery that was kept secret for long ages but has now been disclosed and through the prophetic writings has been made

11. Barnhouse, *Expositions of Bible Doctrines*, 171.

known to all nations, according to the command of the eternal
God, to bring about the obedience of faith—to the only wise God
be glory forevermore through Jesus Christ! Amen.

Paul's benediction is in praise of God's wisdom and power; what God
is doing in the preaching of the gospel of his Son to all people of every
nation, and the existence of this multiracial and diverse church as a manifestation of God's wisdom. Who else could unite around the communion
table: master and slave, male and female, barbarian and Greek, former
worshippers of Yahweh with former worshippers of Zeus?[12] Who else could
pull off the undoing of the curse at Babel, than the one who divided the
nations at one time for their own good?

Through the gospel of Jesus Christ, the curse of division (racial, economic, and sexual) is now starting to be reversed in the church. And in
the end, there will be gathered a numberless multitude from every nation,
from all tribes and peoples and languages, standing before the throne and
before the Lamb, clothed in white robes, with palm branches in their hands,
crying out with a loud voice, "Salvation belongs to our God who sits on the
throne, and to the Lamb" (Rev 7:9, 10). And at the marriage feast of the
Lamb they will cry out like the roar of many waters, "Hallelujah! For the
Lord our God the Almighty reigns" (Rev 19:6). This chorus begins now
in the church, unified into a brotherhood that transcends anything in this
world, glued together by love and the gospel. This should be the pattern and
anything that seeks to delete this picture is going against the very grain of
the gospel and is mocking the very reason for the sacrifice of Jesus Christ!

. . . to the only wise God be glory forevermore through Jesus
Christ! Amen.

---

12. Barnhouse, *Expositions*, 173.

Appendix One

Major Interpretations of Romans 11:25–26

THEORY #1: THE END-TIME THEORY

. . . until the fullness of the gentiles has come in, and then (houtos) all Israel will be saved. After the time of the gentiles, just before the return of Christ, a great mass of Jewish people will be saved.

MY CRITIQUE OF THIS VIEW

1. *houtos*—*so, thus, or in like manner,* not *then or after that.* It emphasizes that there is one covenant of salvation, not two, and the Jews become saved by the same way as the gentiles.

2. The context does not have reference to a future event but something that includes the present.

3. We are not expecting every Jew to be saved, just like we don't expect every gentile to be saved. All along Paul has stressed a remnant.

4. In verses 26–27, a Deliverer is mentioned who will *turn away godlessness and remove sin from Jacob.* This has more to do with Christ's first coming than his second.

THEORY #2: CALVIN'S THEORY

According to this theory, *all Israel* refers to the total number of elect throughout history who are ultimately saved—both Jew and gentile.

> I extend the word Israel to all the people of God, according to this meaning: when the Gentiles shall come in, the Jews also will return from their defection to the obedience of faith, and thus will be completed the salvation of the whole Israel of God, which must be gathered from both.[1]

MY CRITIQUE

1. Although the olive tree metaphor describes the people of God, and Paul in Galatians 6:16 calls the church the *Israel of God*, in this context (vv. 25–26) Israel must not be spiritualized but allowed to mean Israel.

2. Paul uses the term *Israel* eleven times in Romans 9–11, and in every case he means the Jews.

3. Not until verses 30–32 does Paul come back to the entire body of the elect, Jew and gentile.

THEORY #3: THE SUM TOTAL OF THE ELECT JEWS THEORY

All Israel parallels *the fullness of the gentiles. All Israel* means the sum of all the believing Jewish remnant from every age. Just as God is in the process of saving the elect of the gentiles in every age, so he is in the process of doing the same among the Jews and will continue until *all Israel* will be saved. Berkhof says, "All Israel is to be understood as a designation not of the whole nation but of the whole number of elect out of the ancient covenant people."[2]

1. Calvin, *Commentaries on Acts, Romans,* 437.
2. Berkhof, *Systematic Theology,* 699.

MY CRITIQUE OF THIS VIEW

It does not do justice to the buildup that Paul initiates at the beginning of chapter 9—the desire for the salvation of his kinsmen, the Jews, in spite of the blindness that seems to be on Israel in the present time.

THEORY #4: REMOVING THE HARDNESS IN THE FUTURE THEORY

And so all Israel will be saved refers to a time when the partial hardening of Israel will be taken away and God will go beyond saving the characteristic remnant of Israel to saving a majority of national Israel. "*All Israel* is a recurring expression in Jewish literature, where it does not mean every Jew without a single exception, but Israel as a whole."[3] The remainder of verses 26–27 indicates that this salvation will come to Israel on the basis of faith in Christ, not the two-covenant theory offered by Krister Stendahl that gentiles and the remnant of Israel are saved by faith in Christ, while national Israel is saved through their own covenant.[4] Thus the plan of God will not be completed until it embraces all people in the new covenant by means of the gospel of Jesus Christ.

MY CRITIQUE OF THIS VIEW

I believe this fits best the build-up in the context of Romans 11, preserves the importance of the proclamation of the gospel in Romans 10, and keeps the thrust of electing grace begun by Paul in Romans 9.

3. Bruce, "Epistle to the Romans," 222.
4. Stendahl, *Paul*, 4.

Appendix Two

Guide for Individual Study and Group Discussion, Part One

I. PAUL GREETS THE CHURCH AT ROME (1:1–15)

vv. 1–7: Greetings

- How does Paul describe himself to the Romans in this section?

- What can you learn about Jesus from vv. 3–5, which may have been an early creed or hymn? (How about some of you musicians setting it to music for us to sing?)

- Notice any words that are repeated in this section?

vv. 8–15: Paul's Desire to Visit Rome

- What do you learn about the Roman Church and Paul's attitude towards it?

- Why do you think Paul wants to go to Rome? (Look at Romans 15:23–29 and compare it with what really happened in Acts 20:22—28.)

- Notice all the "I" statements in this section. What do they tell you about Paul?

II. PAUL'S THEME (1:16–17)

- Why do you think he mentions not being ashamed of the gospel?

- What kind of power does Paul have in mind?

- At first, he says salvation is to all who believe and then he seems to make a distinction between Jew and gentile. What do you make of that?

- The gospel reveals a righteousness that is from God. What does this mean?

- "The righteous (justified one) shall live by faith." Unpack this statement and put it in your own words as if you were explaining it to a neighbor.

III. A. THE GUILT OF THE GENTILE WORLD (1:18–32)

vv. 18–20: The Wrath of God

- What do you think of when you hear the expression, "the wrath of God"? (Notice that here it is in the present tense.) Why are these people under God's wrath?

- In what ways do you think that the being and nature of God are revealed through creation?

- Do you think Paul means that there is enough evidence for God's existence in creation for people to become Christians? (Learn the difference between general revelation and special revelation.)

vv. 21–32: The Cultural Impact of Unbelief

- Once a person recognizes who God is, what should be his/her proper twofold response?

- When people refuse to recognize God, what happens to their intellect and worship? (Note the word "exchange" in v. 23.)

- When people refuse to recognize God, what happens to the understanding of their hearts? (Note another "exchange" in v. 25.)

- When a person/culture refuses to recognize God, what happens to sexuality within that culture? (Note another "exchange" in v. 26.)

- When a person/culture refuses to recognize God, what happens to the values and relationships within that culture? (Compare this passage to the nightly news.)

v. 24, v. 26, v. 28: The Wrath of God Defined

- What phrase is repeated in these three passages? What does this tell you about the nature of God's wrath that is being revealed from heaven?

- Chew on this one: How can people be held accountable for their sins when they never heard the truth about God?

III. B. THE GUILT OF THE MORAL WORLD (2:1–18)

- In the previous chapter, Paul was describing the wretchedness of pagan culture, which had no standards of morality. In this section, to whom do you think Paul was writing?

- Describe some of the characteristics of these people.

- What is the standard of judgment that God will use in the Final Judgment?

  vv. 9–10

vv. 12–13

vv. 16

- Does it seem to you that Paul is advocating a salvation through good works?

- If you think so, examine the context once again. Is he talking about rejecting the gospel or is he talking about why people are accountable to God and are without excuse (compare with 3:23)?

THINKING MORE DEEPLY

I am a moral person from the tribe of Bongo-Bongo, which is on the coast of Nambi-Pambi. I have lived a good life on the basis of the laws of my culture but I have never heard of the Ten Commandments. Let's say I died and am standing before God in judgment. Let's also say that I had a speech prepared that went something like this: "God, how can you condemn me as a sinner when I did not know you existed nor what you expected of me. I never had the Bible in my language and never heard of the Ten Commandments. I appeal to you to consider my righteousness according to my cultural laws and accept me though ignorant of your laws." What do you think would God say to me on the basis of what have studied so far?

III. C. THE GUILT OF THE JEWISH RELIGIOUS WORLD (2:17—3:8)

- This is the first time Paul addresses the Jews directly: what are the privileges that are theirs?

- How does Paul "pull the rug out from under them" by confronting them with their failure?

- What are the parallels to circumcision today that might give people a false sense of security in their relationship with God?

- How does Paul define a "Jew"?

III. D. UNIVERSAL GUILT BEFORE GOD (3:9-20)

- There are several Greek words that define humanity's sinful response to God. Which ones best fit your own journey to forgiveness?

- What are three things that stand out to you about Paul's diagnostic x-ray of the human condition?

- How should we respond to this diagnosis?

IV. A. RIGHT STANDING WITH GOD PROVIDED BY FAITH (3:21-31)

- How would you define the "righteousness of God"?

- How would you define "justification" and "sanctification"? Does one flow from the other?

- How do you understand the concept of divine forbearance and the "passing over" of the sin of the Old Testament believer?

- What is the difference between "atoning sacrifice" and the term "propitiation"?

IV. B. RIGHT STANDING WITH GOD PROVEN BY THE EXAMPLE OF ABRAHAM (4:1-25)

- Put into your own words how one is declared "in the right" with God.

- Why do you think Paul reaches back into the Old Testament and picks two old guys as illustrations of how we can be put right with God (4:1-8)?

- Do you notice a word that is repeated several times in this section (and in the entire chapter)?

- What do you think it means that Abraham's faith was credited (reckoned, counted) as righteousness?

- What point is Paul making about David? (Hint: What is the blessedness of being put right with God?)

- When was Abraham declared righteous, before or after his circumcision (4:9–16)?

- Why is this timing issue so important to Paul's argument?

- In verse 15, what is the relationship between the law and sin? (Compare 5:13–14, 7:7–13.)

- Underline the phrases in this section that show how incapable Abraham was of fulfilling God's promise in his own power (4:17–25).

- How does this relate to our being "in the right" with God (vv. 23–25)?

IV. C. THE FRUIT OF JUSTIFICATION (5:1-11)

- What are the four pieces of fruit mentioned that are the result of our justification?

- Why is the assurance of our salvation so essential to our spiritual growth?

- What does Paul say is the relationship between suffering and joy?

- What are the subjective and objective proofs of God's love for us?

- What is the key word in 5:9–11? Keep this word in mind and see how it relates to the content of the next section.

IV. D. THE OBEDIENCE OF CHRIST (5:12-21)

- Go back and read verses 12, 18–21 for a summation of Paul's main thought. What are the key principles you see in this section?

- Using a Matryoshka doll, explain Paul's thought to someone else.

- Now read the entire section, including the digression in verses 13–17. Make a list with Adam on one side and Christ on the other. Now compare and contrast the actions and consequences of each as the representatives of the old and new humanities. I'll start you off: under Adam write "one act of disobedience"; under Christ write "one act of obedience."

PRACTICAL APPLICATION

If a friend is facing a crisis of faith because of a difficult situation and asks you this question: "If God created such a good world, why do death and suffering exist?" How would you answer her or him on the basis of what you've learned in this passage?

V. A. THE REIGN OF SIN BROKEN BY OUR DEATH (6:1–14)

- What does it mean to die to sin, and according to Paul how have we died?

- Do you agree with this statement: Paul is not denying the impossibility of sin but the incongruity of sin in the life of the believer?

- How are you dealing with the "old landlord" in your life?

V. B. THE REIGN OF SIN BROKEN BY BECOMING SLAVES TO GOD (6:15–23)

- How is the question in verse 15 similar to or different than in verse 1?

- Put Paul's response in verse 16 into your own words.

- How do Matthew 6:24 and John 8:33–34 relate to what Paul says in verses 16–18?

- Compare the meaning of verse 19 with verse 14. What is the point of each verse?

PRACTICAL APPLICATION

What are three practical ways that seeing yourself as "the slave of God" would make a difference in the way you lived?

V. C. THE BELIEVER'S RELATIONSHIP TO THE LAW (7:1–6)

- Put the principle contained in the last half of verse 1 in your own words.

- What is the point of his example of marriage in verses 2–3?

- Who is the old husband that Paul has in mind? Who do you think the new husband would be? (vv. 4–6) What kind of offspring is produced in relationship to each?

- In the section 6:1—7:6, Paul has used three images: death, slavery, and marriage. Which one helps you to best understand your relationship to Christ?

V. D. THE PURPOSE OF THE MORAL LAW IN THE LIFE OF THE BELIEVER (7:7–13)

- What are the three purposes or effects of the Moral Law that Paul mentions in verses 7–9?

- What is the significance of the change in pronouns and verb tenses in verses 7–13?

- Who or what did Paul discover was the real culprit in his pre-Christian attempt to be religious?

PRACTICAL APPLICATION:

Is your relationship with Christ like a marriage to someone who really loves you or does it seem like no amount of performance will ever please your spouse? Why?

V. E. THE BELIEVER'S STRUGGLE WITH THE REMNANT OF THE OLD NATURE (7:14–25)

- Do you believe that Paul is speaking of his struggle with sin as a believer?

- What does he mean that the law is spiritual but he is unspiritual (literally, "composed of flesh")?

- Can you identify with his struggle in verses 15–19? Can you put these verses into your own words?

- Does verse 17 sound more like an excuse or a confession?

- Remember, Paul states his struggle in 7:14–17 and then repeats himself in 7:18–20:

- Compare verse 14 with verse 1 8. What is the initial assessment of his struggle?

- Compare verse 15 with verse 19. What is the confusion that his struggle produces?

- Compare verses 16–17 with verse 20. What is the discovery that he makes about his struggle?

- What are the two simultaneous cries that Paul utters and what do each indicate about the solution to his dilemma?

PRACTICAL APPLICATION

Joe was under the impression that once he became a Christian it would be easy to deal with his old issues of sin and temptation. But he finds himself still struggling with many of these same issues. In addition, he experiences increased guilt because he feels he should be above these struggles. How would you help Joe on the basis of Paul's teaching in this section?

VI. A. THE MINISTRY OF THE HOLY SPIRIT (8:1–27)

- How is this chapter related to 7:24–25?

- How is the Holy Spirit's work related to the fact that there is no condemnation in the believer's relationship with God?

- In verses 5–9, what are the characteristics of the believer's life compared to that of the unbeliever?

- In what ways have you sensed the Holy Spirit witnessing to your spirit that you are God's child?

- Why do you think Paul links suffering with glory in verses 18–27?

- How many groans do you see in this passage? How many of them have you experienced?

VI. B. THE STEADFAST LOVE OF THE LORD (8:28-39)

- Are there times that you have felt that verse 28 was not appropriate for you to hear?

- What does Paul state as the ultimate reason for why things happen to us (v. 29)?

PRACTICAL APPLICATION

How would you minister to Sally from 8:28–29 as she is facing one of the most tragic situations a person can imagine—the loss of her dad? She is a believer struggling with God's love because he allowed this to happen.

VII. A. THE REJECTION OF ETHNIC ISRAEL AND GOD'S SOVEREIGNTY (9:1-29)

- What is the issue here that makes it look like God's covenant promises to Israel have failed?

- What are two things that we need to remember when it comes to God's election?

- Why can we not charge God with injustice when it comes to having mercy for some and not others?

VII. B. THE REJECTION OF ETHNIC ISRAEL AND HER REJECTION OF CHRIST (9:30—10:21)

- Ethnic Israel's temporary rejection is not only due to God's election, but what else?

- What is the relationship between Israel's rejection of the gospel and the establishment of her own righteousness?

- Why does Paul talk about the absolute importance of evangelism in the context of God's election?

- Why is it that ethnic Israel still doesn't believe?

- How do you personally work through the issue of what happens to those people who have never heard the gospel?

VII. C. AND D. THE REJECTION OF ETHIC ISRAEL IS NOT COMPLETE OR FINAL (11:1–36)

- What is the evidence that Paul gives to show that God has not rejected national Israel?

- How do you understand the process of judicial hardening?

- Draw a picture of verses 17–24. Make it as complete as possible following Paul's thought.

- How do you understand verses 25–26—that "all Israel will be saved"? (See Appendix One.)

- What evidence can you find in Romans demonstrating that the salvation of "all Israel" will be based upon faith in Jesus Christ and not on the basis of a separate covenant?

Appendix Three

Guide for Individual Study and Group Discussion, Part Two

I.A. IN A LIFE OF CONSECRATION (2:1-2)

- What is the basis of Paul's appeal to surrender?

- Why is the use of the term *body* important to Paul's sacrificial language?

- How expansive is Paul's use of the term *worship*?

- What are some examples of conformity to the world with which you have struggled?

- How important is the mind in the process of one's spiritual development?

- Is your understanding of God's will more geographical or relational?

I.B. IN A HUMBLE AND CARING MINISTRY
WITHIN THE CHURCH (12:3–21)

- Do you know what your spiritual gift is? Have others affirmed this gift in you?

- Why is realistic thinking about your place in the body of Christ so important?

- Can you think of one example of a time when you experienced genuine love, and one example of when you showed it to someone else?

- Why do you think verse 18 is especially important to our relationships? How do you understand the "heaping burning coals on the head" passage?

I.C. IN THE REALITIES OF POLITICAL
AND SOCIAL LIFE (13:1–7)

- In what way does Paul see governing authorities as "ministers of God"?

- What are our bottom-line responsibilities to the state, according to this text? Does Peter add anything in 1 Peter 2:13–17?

- Do you tend toward the position of pacifism or toward activism? What is the chief danger of your position?

- How would you have dealt with the National Socialist government as a Christian in Nazi Germany? Do you agree with Bonhoeffer's change of conscience?

I.D. THE DEBT OF LOVE (13:8–14)

- How does Paul use a financial term to describe the kind of relationship that should exist between believers?

- In what way is Paul's understanding of love a fulfillment of the law?

- What does this love really look like?

- Why do you think Paul brings in the concept of the imminent return of Christ?

I.E. IN THE FELLOWSHIP OF BELIEVERS FROM DIVERSE CULTURES (14:1—15:13)

- What are some of the scruples over which Christians disagree today?

- What was the issue that Paul was addressing in the church at Rome?

- How would you define "the weak" and "the strong"?

- Paul gives us an excellent test of our scruples. What is it?

- Why should we be careful when exercising our Christian freedom?

- What is your personal response to the hypothetical situation about drinking wine in this section?

- How do you understand the difference between trying to please others and being a people-pleaser?

- How would you have handled the situation with the African brother who liked to sing?

- What is the ultimate purpose of Christian unity?

II.A. PAUL'S HEART AND CALLING (15:14-22)

- Describe Paul's heart:

- Describe Paul's desire:

- Describe Paul's ambition:

- Describe Paul's strategy:

- What is your strategy at this stage of your life?

II.B. PAUL'S PLAN TO VISIT ROME (15:23–33)

- After revealing his desire to visit Rome on his way to Spain, Paul said he had to do something first that was going to take him out of his way. What was it?

- What was the significance of this offering? (Make sure you read 1 Corinthians 16:1–4; 2 Corinthians 8, 9 as background.)

- Paul finally got to Rome, but did so by means beyond his control. (Read Acts 21–28 for background and to see God's sovereign hand at work.)

- Have you ever strived together with someone in prayer? What does that mean to you?

II.C. TO THE ONLY WISE GOD (16:1–27)

- What did you learn about Paul and the early church in chapter 16?

- What did you learn about yourself and some of your own prejudice?

- In what ways can we say that Satan is alive, but not well?

- In what ways does our culture honor diversity in a way that polarizes and fuels animosity?

- How is and how will the glory and wisdom of God be demonstrated?

Bibliography

Anderson, N. T. *The Bondage Breaker*. Eugene, OR: Harvest, 1993.

Augustine. *The Confessions of St. Augustine*. Translated by Edward Pusey. Kila: Kessinger, 2012. Kindle ed.

Barnhouse, D. G. *Expositions of Bible Doctrines: Taking the Epistle to the Romans as a Point of Departure*. 4 vols. Grand Rapids: Eerdmans, 1952–64.

Barrett, C. K. *A Commentary on the Epistle to the Romans*. Black's New Testament Commentary. London: A. & C. Black, 1957.

Barth, Karl. *The Epistle to the Romans*. 6th ed. Oxford: Oxford University Press, 1933.

Berkhof, Louis. *Systematic Theology*. Grand Rapids: Eerdmans, 1968.

Bolton, Samuel. *The True Bounds of Christian Freedom*. Edinburgh: Banner of Truth, 1964.

Bonar, Horatius. "Not What These Hands Have Done." https://hymnary.org/text/not_what_these_hands_have_done.

Bonhoeffer, Dietrich. *Ethics*. New York: Macmillan, 1957.

Boston, Thomas. *Human Nature in Its Fourfold State*. Edinburgh: Banner of Truth, 1964.

Bray, Gerald L., ed. *The Ancient Christian Commentary on Scripture*. Vol. 6, *New Testament: Romans*. Downers Grove: InterVarsity, 2001.

Bruce, F. F. "Epistle to the Romans." In *Zondervan Pictorial Encyclopedia of the Bible*, edited by Merrill Tenney, 163–82. Grand Rapids: Zondervan, 1975.

———. *Letter of Paul to the Romans: An Introduction and Commentary*. The Tyndale New Testament Commentary Series 6. Grand Rapids: Eerdmans, 1963.

Calvin, John. *Commentaries on Acts 14–28, Romans 1–16*. Calvin's Commentaries 19. Grand Rapids: Baker, 1979.

———. *Commentaries on Galatians, Ephesians, Philippians, Colossians, Thessalonians, Timothy, Titus, and Philemon*. Calvin's Commentaries 21. Grand Rapids: Baker, 1979.

———. *Institutes of the Christian Religion: A New Translation*. Translated by Henry Beveridge. Grand Rapids: Eerdmans, 1966.

Chalmers, Thomas. *The Expulsive Power of a New Affection*. Minneapolis: Curiosmith, 2012.

Conzelmann, Hans. *Gentiles, Jews, Christians: Polemics and Apologetics in the Greco-Roman Era*. Translated by M. Eugene Boring. Minneapolis: Fortress, 1992.

Cranfield, C. E. B. *Romans: A Shorter Commentary*. Grand Rapids: Eerdmans, 1985.

Denney, James. *St. Paul's Epistle to the Romans.* The Expositor's Greek New Testament 2. Grand Rapids: Eerdmans, 1970.

Dodd, C. H. *The Epistle of Paul to the Romans.* The Moffat New Testament Commentary. London: Hodder & Stoughton, 1932.

Donfried, Karl P. *The Romans Debate.* Peabody: Hendrickson, 1991.

Dunn, J. D. G. *Romans.* Word Biblical Commentary 38A–B. Dallas: Word, 1988.

Fee, Gordon D. *God's Empowering Presence: The Holy Spirit in the Letters of Paul.* Peabody: Hendrickson, 1994.

Glasser, Arthur F. "The Apostle Paul and the Missionary Task." In *Perspectives on the World Christian Movement: A Reader,* edited by Ralph D. Winter and Steven C. Hawthorne, 149–53. 4th ed. Pasadena: Carey, 2009.

Godet, Frédéric. *Commentary on the Epistle to the Romans.* 2 vols. New York: Funk & Wagnalls, 1886.

Haldane, Robert. *The Epistle to the Romans.* Geneva Series of Commentaries. Edinburgh: The Banner of Truth, 1958.

Harrison, Graham S., et al. *The Christian and the State in Revolutionary Times.* The Westminster Conference. Grand Rapids; Baker, 1975.

Hendrikson, William. *New Testament Commentary: Romans.* Grand Rapids: Baker, 1981.

Herndon, Booton. *Hero of Hacksaw Ridge.* Coldwater, MD: Remnant, 2016.

Hodge, Charles H. *A Commentary on Romans.* Geneva Series of Commentaries, London: Banner of Truth, 1972.

Jewitt, Robert. *Christian Tolerance: Paul's Message to the Modern Church.* Philadelphia: Westminster, 1982.

Kasemann, Ernst. *Commentary on Romans.* London: SCM, 1980.

King, Martin Luther, Jr. *Letter from a Birmingham Jail.* https://www.africa.upenn.edu/Articles_Gen/Letter_Birmingham.html.

Liddon, Henry Parry. *Explanatory Analysis of St. Paul's Epistle to the Romans.* Grand Rapids: Zondervan, 1961.

Luther, Martin. *Commentary on the Epistle to the Romans.* Translated by J. T. Mueller. Grand Rapids: Zondervan, 1954.

———. "Preface to the Complete Edition of Luther's Latin Writings (1545)." Translated by Lewis Spitz, Jr. In *Luther's Works,* vol. 34, American Edition. Philadelphia: Muhlenberg, 1960.

Marshall, I. Howard. *The Book of Acts: An Introduction and Commentary.* Tyndale New Testament Commentaries 5. Grand Rapids: Eerdmans, 1980.

McGowan, A. T. B. *Adam, Christ and Covenant: Exploring Headship Theology.* London: Apollos, 2016.

Metaxis, Eric. *Martin Luther: The Man Who Rediscovered God and Changed The World.* New York: Viking, 2017.

Moo, D. *The Epistle to The Romans.* The New International Commentary of the New Testament. Grand Rapids: Eerdmans, 1996.

Morris, Leon. *The Epistle to the Romans.* Pillar New Testament Commentary. Grand Rapids: Eerdmans, 1988.

Murray, J. *The Epistle to the Romans.* The New International Commentary on the New Testament. Grand Rapids: Eerdmans, 1968.

Ortlund, Raymond C., Jr. *A Passion for God: Prayers and Meditations on the Book of Romans.* Wheaton: Crossway, 1994.

Owen, John. *Temptation and Sin.* Grand Rapids: Sovereign Grace, 1971.

Peterson, Eugene H. *The Message: The New Testament in Contemporary English*. Colorado Springs: NavPress, 1993.

Pillai, K. C. *Light through an Eastern Window*. New York: Speller, 1963.

Plantinga, Cornelius, Jr. *Not the Way It's Supposed to Be: A Breviary of Sin*. Grand Rapids: Eerdmans, 1995.

Richardson, Don. *Eternity in Their Hearts*. Ventura: Regal, 1981.

Schaeffer, Francis A. *The Church at the End of the Twentieth Century*. Downers Grove: InterVarsity, 1970.

Schreiner, Thomas R. *Romans*. The Baker Exegetical Commentary on the New Testament. Grand Rapids: Baker, 1998.

Sproul, R. C. *Faith Alone: Evangelical Doctrine of Justification*. Grand Rapids: Baker, 1995.

Steele, D. N., and C. C. Thomas. *Romans: An Interpretive Outline*. Philadelphia: Presbyterian and Reformed, 1963.

Stendahl, Krister. *Paul among the Jews and Gentiles and Other Essays*. Philadelphia: Fortress, 1976.

Stott, John R. W. *Romans: God's Good News for the World*. Downers Grove: InterVarsity, 1991.

Tenney, M. C., ed. *The Zondervan Pictorial Encyclopedia of the Bible*. Vol. 5, Q–Z. Grand Rapids: Zondervan, 1975.

van Paassan, Pierre. *That Day Alone*. New York: Dial, 1941.

Wells, David F. *No Place for Truth: Or Whatever Happened to Evangelical Theology?* Grand Rapids: Eerdmans, 1993.

Wesley, Charles. "And Can It Be." https://hymnary.org/text/and_can_it_be_that_i_should_gain.

Wesley, John. *Journal from October 14, 1735, to November 29, 1745*. The Works of John Wesley 1. 3rd ed. Grand Rapids: Baker, 1979.

Wright, N. T. *Justification: God's Plan and Paul's Vision*. Downers Grove: IVP Academic, 2009.

———. *New Tasks for a Renewed Church*. London: Hodder and Stoughton, 1992.

Zacharias, Ravi. *Jesus among Other Gods: The Absolute Claims of the Christian Message*. Nashville: Word, 2000.

CPSIA information can be obtained
at www.ICGtesting.com
Printed in the USA
LVHW010926210420
654166LV00005B/1354

9 781725 252691